HOW TO BE A
(OR A KID WITH SILLY IDEAS)

A GUIDE TO FOSTERING A FORWARD-THINKING MINDSET

ADAM FOLEY

Copyright © 2021
All rights reserved.
ISBN - 9798745536427

Dedicated to my mother for her patience with my wandering mind and inability to keep a silly idea to myself

CONTENTS

INTRODUCTION 7
   The Origin 7
   The Book 10
   The Author 12

CHAPTER 1: PUT IN THE WORK 15
   My First Futurist... 15
   Scene 1: A Child with Passion 17
   Scene 2: A Chance Encounter 18
   Balancing the Effort Beam 21

CHAPTER 2: COURAGE TO PERSISTENTLY SHARE YOUR IDEA 23
   Scene 3: Am I Crazy?... 23
   Scene 4: The Approach 24
   Scene 5: The Epilogue... 27
   The Anti-Dave 28
   Board Room Judgement 29
   Summing it Up 32

CHAPTER 3: EAGERNESS TO RALLY AGAINST THE STATUS QUO 34
   A Childhood Change Agent 34
   Progress Takes People.. 36
   Lifting Up Others 40
   Creating a Movement 42
   Challenging @ the Office... 44

CHAPTER 4: TAKE ACTION 49

An Inspirational Icon 49
Following a Vision Takes Work 51
Activist Futurism 54
Getting Bored is a Good Thing 55
CHAPTER 5: HAVE FUN WITH IT 57
Mr. Smith Goes to the Web 57
An Entertaining Visionary 59
The Jovial Billionaire 63
Balance in All Things 65
CHAPTER 6: FOSTER CREATIVITY 70
Creative Practicality 70
Consultant-Painter / Painter-Consultant 73
How Creativity Works 75
Give Yourself Permission to be Creative 77
Fall in Love with Being a Generalist 79
Generalism in Action 81
Get Comfortable with Being Uncomfortable 83
An Unfinished Journey 85
CHAPTER 7: FIND A PARTNER 88
The Lonely Futurist 88
The Benefit of Abrasion 91
The Wisdom of Raj 92
Ideation Requires Variation 94
CHAPTER 8: NEVER SAY NEVER 97
My Origin Story 97
To Boldly Go 98
Never is a "No-No" Word 100

Beyond Impossible 102
Never in the Day to Day 105
CHAPTER 9: PREPARE FOR AND LEARN FROM MISTAKES 107
Professorial Wisdom 107
Plan and be Humble 109
Coaching through Disruption 111
Wii Were Wrong 112
CONCLUSION: PULLING IT ALL TOGETHER 115
The CliffsNotes 115
The Final Word 117

INTRODUCTION

The Origin

As a child, I was known for my outlandish ideas about the world around me. My sentences would often start with "One day..." followed by a declarative statement:

- "Instead of food, we'll take a pill that will give us all we need for the day"
- "We'll have metal roads that replace concrete ones that keep cracking"
- "There will be floating stores that will come to you instead of you going to them"

They weren't perfect predictions, but they did identify problems that needed to be addressed, and even had the seeds of plausible ideas within them. My adult-self will claim the above are child-like forecasts of meal replacement products like Soylent (food pill), advancements in materials science (metal roads), and online shopping (floating stores) – and I'm sticking to it!

On a day I was feeling particularly antagonistic, my mother had suggested I work on my spelling – something I had been struggling with at the time (my test scores quantified this quite well). With great confidence, I retorted "in the future, this will get figured out – technology will be able to fix my spelling, so I'll never have to be that good!" I believe my mother laughed, rolled her eyes, and told me to get back to my homework. However, this was a prediction that I nailed. Today, I still live and breathe by the squiggly red line.

At the time, the term "futurist" had yet to make it into mainstream vocabulary[1], but looking back on my life, I have always been one. There are few activities I enjoy more than identifying a problem, coming up with wild conjectures about how future events or technology might handle them, debating the idea with others, and working the concept until it is either shelved as illogical or upgraded to "not a bad idea".

---

[1] Futurist (noun), "Someone who studies and predicts events in the future. There are many different kinds of futurists, from scientists who forecast the future effects of climate change to marketers who try to anticipate what teenagers will be desperate to spend money on in five years". https://www.vocabulary.com/dictionary/futurist
(accessed 15 August 2020).

During a camping trip in the summer of 2019, isolated from major forms of technology and struggling to sleep, I ironically started reflecting on technology and on how I wound up developing a passion for futurism as well as a relatively decent batting average with making predictions about trends and events. I soon came to the realization that there was no formal training manual on the topic or curriculum to guide my journey into the world of futurism. I simply stumbled into it.

While today there are some available options such as courses from Singularity University (I have a certificate from one such program), I noticed there was a gap in written content. There are endless books and reports produced by research and consulting firms written on "the future of [insert industry]"; however, there are very few written on how to develop the mindset behind a futurist or the fundamental ways of taking an idea from a fleeting thought into a well-developed concept that the general population can open their minds to.

Shortly after this I decided to write a LinkedIn article with the same title as this book. After compressing ideas I've had for years into 900 words, I realized I had more to say on the topic. It is with that purpose that I decided to write this book.

The Book

While there is plenty of research and methodology behind making sophisticated predictions about the future, the focus of this book will be on honing the personality traits required to be an effective futurist and forward-thinker. The book itself is not intended as an instruction guide or manual on futurism, but rather a source that I hope is thought provoking and might spark a futurist journey within both a well-seasoned working professional and a child dreaming of floating buildings.

I have a personal grudge against non-fiction books that drag on for more pages and chapters than necessary to convey a message, so you will find that the book itself is short and sweet. Because of this, I have hyper-footnoted (not a word, I know) each chapter with references so that you can dive deeper into topics of interest at your discretion. Footnotes will also include some of my meandering thoughts that are not entirely essential to the key messages.

Within each chapter, we will explore a specific principle that I believe is essential to envisioning the future, and perhaps more importantly, conveying your vision to an audience. The content within this book is structured around a series of interviews with and stories about individuals throughout my life that I believe embody positive futurist traits. Coupled with personal anecdotes, historical events, and case studies, this book is part informational, part inspirational, and part a tribute to those people who have influenced my personal and professional life. While you can certainly jump from chapter to chapter to whichever theme you find most relevant, it was designed as a story, and as such, is recommended to read from cover to cover the first time through.

My hope is that this book can serve a catalyst for forward-thinkers and dreamers to put their ideas on paper, push the envelope, and build something new and exciting. While I do not imagine my path will take me to create the next SpaceX or Amazon, my dream is that someone reading this book one day will.

The Author

While this book is designed to address to some degree my personal and professional background through references to experiences, life lessons, and redacted client engagements, I would be remiss if I did not provide some additional background.

I grew up around technology throughout my early life. My father is a software engineer, and I think we were the only family in the neighborhood with a server in our basement. As will be discussed during the book, I have always enjoyed opening my mind to new ideas, and while it would seem natural for me to pursue engineering or hard sciences, I had yet to come to the realization of my love for both these things when pursuing a college degree. Following in my brother's footsteps, I wound up pursuing a business degree with a focus in strategy, accounting, and information technology.

Since graduating from the University of Michigan Ross School of Business[2], I had been a professional management

---

[2] Go Blue!

consultant[3] focused on technology for most of my career. Across almost a decade, I have helped Fortune 500 companies, start-ups, non-profits, and governments figure out what they need to do with technology to survive, and hopefully thrive, in a rapidly changing world.

Sometimes that work has required pie in the sky visioning – at other times, very practical, operational advice. As a result, I learned to thrive bouncing between both imaginative and realistic views of the world. I now work in the internal strategy department of one company – dedicating my time to pushing the frontier of how we drive new capabilities within our organization and use technology, not just as a tool to keep operations humming, but one that can bring value and drive the business strategy forward.

I am constantly on the hunt for new knowledge. This drive has led me to obtain my MBA, certifications in analytics, an array of technological standards, emerging technologies such as blockchain, and less directly applicable credentials in modern and contemporary art, genetics, and the science of

---

[3] If you're unfamiliar with the vagueness that is such a career title, you can start here: https://en.wikipedia.org/wiki/Management_consulting. For everyone else that is completely disinterested, just insert "corporate problem solver for hire" every time you see me reference my career throughout this book.

happiness[4]. I am also a 3D printing enthusiast, "had too much time on my hands during the pandemic" abstract artist, and outer space nerd (you'll hear more about this later) who hopes one day he'll retire on the moon, Mars, or perhaps hurtling through space in cryosleep on the way to a distant star system[5].

I have been known to play devil's advocate more often than I advocate for my own perspectives, and I strongly believe the abrasion of contrary ideas is a healthy and important part of learning and growth (even if it can sometimes lead to frustration among my friends and family).

I hope you enjoy what I've written in the subsequent pages, and if you do not, in the spirit of my previous comments openly welcome criticism to incorporate into a subsequent edition!

---

[4] This is an excellent certification and free class through Coursera facilitated by Laurie Santos from Yale University – I would highly recommend it to anyone interested in exploring what does and does not drive well-being and happiness from a scientific perspective: https://www.coursera.org/learn/the-science-of-well-being

[5] Baggaley, Kate. "'Cryosleep' May Open the Door to Deep Space. Here's How." *NBC News*. 12 June 2017 https://www.nbcnews.com/mach/tech/cryosleep-may-be-key-deep-space-missions-here-s-how-ncna770961 (accessed 9 August 2020).

CHAPTER 1:

PUT IN THE WORK

My First Futurist

I grew up in the suburbs of Detroit in a town called Northville. With an actively preserved Victorian aesthetic for the past hundred years, Northville holds its central corridor to the strictest of guidelines for how each storefront will look and feel, from its signage all the way to its pastel color palette. During the town's annual "Victorian Festival[6]", the celebration of 19th century heritage goes further still with men adorning paperboy hats, suspenders, and wool pants, and women wrapped in ostentatious hoop dresses. It is somewhat ironic that this town focused on memorializing the past would be where I would be galvanized as a futurist.

A community of around 20,000 people, Northville's social structure centers around families taking care of each other. When someone's parents went out of town, they would send their children to another family for the weekend. When

---

[6] *Northville Heritage Festival.* https://www.northville.org/northville-heritage-festival (accessed 9 August 2020)

grandparents became ill or passed away, families would rally to deliver food to help ease burdens and show support. It was in this social support structure where I met the father of one of these households and the first futurist of my life, David Rabahy (I still call him Mr. Rabahy out of respect on most days).

Dave is a man with significant presence. He stands around 6'6" with a lumberjack build and prominent salt and pepper goatee – often adorning a wide-brimmed hat someone might wear in the outback of Australia. This would all be rather intimidating if it weren't for his ever-inviting smile and teddy bear demeanor. Always with a cheerful tone, Dave will engage anyone in conversation about anything. But, if you really want to get him started, you talk about science, technology, and the future. Both fiercely intelligent and family-oriented, Dave is the kind of person you see at an astronomy conference holding the hand of his barely talking-age child pointing out fascinating booths and breaking down the fundamentals of faster than light travel.

He has a presence that invites you in from afar for a casual chat, always extending a broad, open palm for a respectful but warm handshake whether you are in your early teens or your 60s. He talks to everyone he meets with respect, and regardless of background, education, or career, listens intently – even if it is not a topic that is readily stimulating. Always seeking to peel back the onion of a conversation, Dave will often move conversations along with phrases like "now when you say something like that..." or "that's interesting because –".

When I decided I was going to write this book and interview people throughout my life that I thought displayed wonderful futurist attributes, Dave was the first person I thought of. His futurist journey reads a bit like a movie, and it starts with a cheesy flashback.

Scene 1: A Child with Passion

As a child, Dave was always interested in math. Science to a lesser extent, but numbers were really a passion. Teachers and parents alike fostered that interest, but much of his motivation came from within. So, when the first commercial, four function calculators hit the market in the early 70s[7], Dave saved up his hard-earned lawn mowing money and was among the first people to buy one. Not

---

[7] "The History of Calculators: From Adding Machines to Graphing Calculators". *EdTech Magazine*. https://edtechmagazine.com/k12/article/2012/11/calculating-firsts-visual-history-calculators (accessed 9 August 2020)

because he needed it for a job or school, but because he saw the incredible potential in the technology and wanted to be among the first to explore it.

He spent endless hours using his new piece of the modern frontier, but not just calculating tips at the end of a meal. He wanted to know how it worked. So, he invested the time to learn its level of precision, what would cause it to show the error symbol (apparently turning it on and off rapidly), and the logic behind all its functions.

As Dave describes it, his curiosity was "beyond normal" to the point that no one really cared about what he was doing. But for him, those four functions were everything. As you might imagine, when computers hit the market years later, Dave was once again chomping at the bit.

Scene 2: A Chance Encounter

Queue the movie montage, and suddenly it is Christmas of 2011. His son, Paul, who very much like Dave loves exploring new technologies, provides Dave with a physical representation of a Bitcoin and a redemption code for one token in a digital wallet. At the time the coin was valued at about $16...

Reflecting, Dave said "Best Christmas gift I've ever gotten". When I laughed, he said "No, seriously…" This was not just because of the implicit value of that coin today, but because it sparked his curiosity. A curiosity that Dave had been honing for decades. His journey into Bitcoin, as he and I discussed, wasn't an apple falling and hitting you on top of the head moment – it was as he describes a "protracted aha!".

After that Christmas, Dave dove into Bitcoin in the same way he approached the calculator. He didn't want to just buy some speculative notion, he wanted to know everything about it – spending what he estimates was well over 100 hours learning about the organization's governance and potential scenarios that could break the protocol. He joined forums, downloaded and reviewed the code, and started attending enthusiast meet ups – all before he took out a single position more than that initial coin his son gave him.

It was at that point, after all the research, he realized the value of the idea. This ethereal notion of digital cash was going to change humanity. So, he made an investment. Not enough to put retirement at risk, but certainly enough to be committed to the cause and is a stake today worth considerably more than that initial Christmas gift.

We probably all know someone (or have been that someone) who gets swept up in a new trend and invests in a buzz worthy opportunity after reading a brief article or watching the price rocket up and getting FOMO[8] (I've been here myself). We also probably know how this can play out poorly quite quickly and the feeling of embarrassment that follows – coupled with a need to justify how the outcome "wasn't your fault".

I'd argue that most negative investment outcomes come from people who haven't put in the work. Forecasting the future is a lot like picking a stock to invest in, and it's not as simple as following your gut or hunches or convincing pitches – you need to be diligent like Dave.

> **PRINCIPLE #1 – PUT IN THE WORK**
> Preaching a new idea without putting forth the effort to research your concept, the history of adjacent technologies or trends, and others exploring the field makes you just a guesser and risks you becoming a bit of charlatan shilling ideas you thought of in the shower. A true futurist is methodical and puts in the time to become an expert on the theoretical.

---

[8] Fear of missing out

Balancing the Effort Beam

When organizations have asked my previous teams to come up with new ideas or solutions to their most challenging problems, it was tempting to anchor on our credentials as "smart people" for hire. In fact, it's common for consulting companies to put the source at the bottom of a slide "Based on [insert company] experience". This will only get you so far, and will certainly illicit internal groans by the recipient, especially if they ask you to explain, and you simply tell them the exact same thing verbally. This is why it's important to put in the work.

Unless you can prove out your research, the reports you've read, the experts consulted, lectures attended, specific projects you've led, etc., you're going to look like a person who has just reached into a bag of technology buzzword magnets and threw them at a fridge. The wilder the idea, the more support you will need. To aid in this, consultants will often create "by the numbers" slides or infographics that show visually the amount of research that was put into the analysis. Oh, and the more footnotes the better[9] – everyone

---
[9] Why else do you think I have footnotes?

loves a good 10-line footnote section. While you're at it, throw in a 20-page appendix to boot.

Putting in your due diligence is essential to forming any well-developed idea. If you haven't done research, you're just taking wild guesses and will probably have some serious holes poked in your argument or idea the second it meets public scrutiny.

CHAPTER 2:
COURAGE TO PERSISTENTLY SHARE YOUR IDEA

Scene 3: Am I Crazy?

Once a year, I would run into Dave at a Christmas gathering in my hometown with all the families I grew up with[10]. The first year after his "protracted aha!", he was enthusiastically talking about this strange thing called Bitcoin. At the time the concept sounded a bit unreasonable. A digital currency that is not tied to a country or government and was created by mysterious people to shift the notion of value away from centralized organizations[11]. We all kind of laughed it off. Dave was known for his somewhat eccentric passions (prime numbers being one of them), but he is just such an engaging person to talk with that you kind of always want to learn more.

Each subsequent year he'd provide us an update on what he was doing with Bitcoin. Convincing a local ice cream shop

---

[10] Unfortunately, over the years I have not been able to attend all these gatherings given my work schedule and location across the country, but I love them whenever I can attend.
[11] No fancy footnote here, Wikipedia's got you covered: https://en.wikipedia.org/wiki/Bitcoin

to accept the currency. Joining advocate groups seeking to drive adoption. Handing out Bitcoin "nickels" for free to people (my brother included) as a means of introduction to the space. When my brother received said "nickel", it was worth maybe $7-10. It was a small but meaningful gesture to "get it into people's hands" and hope that seed grew into the same passion that emerged when his son provided him his first access point.

Scene 4: The Approach

We spoke at length about what it's like to try and explain far out concepts to people. The core challenge we identified is that most people are very much "stuck in the present" because it is what they experience day-to-day and only see incremental changes from one year to the next. Breaking someone's locked in view of the present and figuring out what level of "abstraction" can connect with them is the goal of being a convincing futurist. This can take some trial and error, and sometimes yields less than encouraging behavior, such as laughter.

As Dave says "being laughed at is okay – you have to be comfortable with that. If you're socially shy… it's going to be a hard time"[12]. But he says he's learned to enjoy it and embraces the persona of a fun-loving nerd that makes him approachable and learns to adapt each time a method or approach fails. When a pitch doesn't work, he takes comfort in knowing that he learned a new data point or anecdote he would need to bring to the table.

Catering to your audience is an essential component of telling a futurist story. So, if someone is visual, draw a picture. If someone is interested in finance, maybe you demonstrate the economics, patterns, and new markets. For someone into history, perhaps the fascinating Bitcoin origin story that is truly something out of a sci-fi hacker film. The point is, Dave sees explaining something futuristic as a challenge to himself, not a burden on the other person to "free their mind"[13] so they can understand.

Dave is a pure futurist. He doesn't shill Bitcoin to try and pump its value (something many people do). He truly was and still is fascinated by the concept and wants to share his

---

[12] I used to have a real problem with this as well – it doesn't come naturally, and you gotta go out of your way to take yourself less seriously and care less about what people think. Thanks Mike (college roommate) for getting me out of my shell.
[13] Reference to "*The Matrix*" (1999) for those too young to have it embedded in their vernacular.

vision[14] with others, and he is willing to try a variety a means to get the point across. He's still working on his mother-in-law, but one day he says he thinks he'll get her onboard.

> **PRINCIPLE #2 – COURAGE TO PERSISTENTLY SHARE YOUR VISION**
>
> It takes guts to open your mouth and share a wild idea with someone due to a natural fear of rejection and judgement – but it takes true courage to be laughed at and take it as an opportunity to overcome the obstacle. To quote Rocky from the 6th installment in the series: *"...it ain't about how hard you hit. It's about how hard you can get hit and keep moving forward; how much you can take and keep moving forward..."*

---

[14] Dave believes fundamentally that a peer-to-peer currency that is not controlled or able to be diluted in value by governments and can transcend borders is an essential evolution (or option) that empowers individuals.

Scene 5: The Epilogue

The role of a futurist is to make his or her audience understand the theory, not expect the audience to just "get it". A failure to convince is never the fault of the recipient, it is a challenge to the futurist to tell the story better. Dave has always abided by this mantra and taken it in stride, and he put in the work to prove his expertise on the subject.

While the jury is out as to whether Bitcoin will fulfill its prophecies of a decentralized, global store of value, when the chairman of the New York Stock Exchange was asked in November 2018 if digital assets would survive, he said "The unequivocal answer is yes". Only time will tell...[15]

---

[15] I had considered making "patience" one of my core futurist principles given how long it can take for a theory to be proven one way or the other (you might not even be alive for it), but I couldn't justify dragging the reader through pages of something their parents probably taught them years ago.

The Anti-Dave

For those of you who know who Richard Dawkins is, you might see where I am headed with this one[16]. Dawkins is the opposite of Dave. Oxford educated, he embodies any pretentious stereotype you may connect with such an institution. Dawkins is also quite combative. Just Google "Richard Dawkins attacks", hit the video tab, and watch any number of videos that pop up[17]. His targets typically focus on religiously devout individuals and telling them their world is fiction, and at times, he has called for "militant atheism" against anyone who doesn't agree with his message on evolution.

While Richard Dawkins is a world-renowned scientist, known for his credentials and publications in biology - he is also an asshole. He enjoys belittling people and making them feel small for not understanding. He doesn't think from other's perspectives or seek to try a different approach to get his message across. He takes criticism incredibly personally and dismissively. I don't know if I've ever seen the man smile.

---

[16] Once again, Wikipedia will suffice here: https://en.wikipedia.org/wiki/Richard_Dawkins
[17] Here, I did it for you: https://bit.ly/33EzHbf

Richard is cold and aloof. Dave is warm and inviting. Be like Dave.

Board Room Judgement

There have been many times in my career that I have been jeered or laughed at. If you tell an organization that you only arrived at five weeks prior, which has existed for decades without you, that they are facing a major threat of being disintermediated from a blockchain, gig-economy world, you tend to get criticized.

Sometimes it is tissue rejection that your idea is too far of a leap. Sometimes it is a defense mechanism that they fear their life's work has been for nothing. And sometimes it's just because you're the youngest person in the room and "who are you" to dare tell them what to do. It is (almost) never personal, and it won't do you any benefit to take it that way. Instead you must step back, assess the opinions in the room, and come at it from a different angle.

During one of my assignments, I was interfacing regularly with a C-suite executive of a Fortune 100 company on an assessment of the disruptive technologies landscape and how it could impact their business. I was still fairly junior at the company, so some pot shots were being taken at me throughout the duration of the project. Comments like "how are you getting so much time with us?" and "you're missing the historical context here" abounded during each of our sessions, but it didn't break my spirit.

It was a challenge for me to prove my worth. So, I doubled my effort, went over my findings with a fine-tooth comb, and honed my pitch. I chocked the report full of a variety of mechanisms designed to resonate with the disparate body of recipients – analogies, external reports, statistics, case studies – anything I could get my hands on. In the end, the project concluded with a great embrace of our findings and further dissemination of the recommendations beyond the department we were engaged with and throughout the entire organization.

It now stands as a pillar of how they view technology and the organization's vision of the future. While my name (and my company's name) are nowhere to be found on the collateral embraced by the organization[18], I am honored to have succeed in putting in the time and persistently sharing my vision with the client.

---

[18] Months later an employee from said organization e-mailed me a copy of my work asking me to read it to "catch up" on the technological trends and issues they were facing...

While it is somewhat foolish to compare myself to Elon Musk, I'm going to do so to drive home a point. In the early 2000s, people laughed at Musk when he said he was going to disrupt the entrenched automotive industry that had previously been in symbiotic harmony for decades, and he persisted. During his persistence, he has employed all sort of methods to convince and captivate the public – including some of his more "off the rails"[19] ideas such as the infamous selling of flamethrowers in 2018. As of April 2021, Tesla is now worth over half a trillion dollars.

Musk genuinely enjoys the "haters"[20] – it lets him know that he's onto something. I am sure he still takes great satisfaction in having convinced the inconvincible to imagine a different world that is slowly becoming reality.

---

[19] This is definitely a hyperloop pun.
[20] Musk put onto the Tesla online store "short shorts" for sale as a means of mocking those analysts and "prophets" who were shorting his stock and predicting Tesla's demise.
"Elon Musk reveals '$69.420' Tesla short shorts". *CNet.* 6 July 2020. https://www.cnet.com/news/elon-musk-reveals-69-420-tesla-short-shorts/. (accessed 9 August 2020).

Summing it Up[21]

While we cannot all have the charismatic warmness Dave embodies, a futurist must do what they can to be convincing without being combative. If you truly want to influence in the times when facts or numbers are failing, try to anchor on the following list from a pithy but accurate piece from *Scientific American*[22]:

1. Keep emotions out of the exchange
2. Discuss, don't attack (no ad hominem and no ad Hitlerum)
3. Listen carefully and try to articulate the other position accurately
4. Show respect
5. Acknowledge that you understand why someone might hold that opinion
6. Try to show how changing facts does not necessarily mean changing worldviews

---

[21] Call back to the whole calculator thing in the beginning… see what I did there…
[22] Shermer, Michael. "How to Convince Someone When Facts Fail". *Scientific American*. 1 January 2017. https://www.scientificamerican.com/article/how-to-convince-someone-when-facts-fail/ (accessed 9 August 2020).

The reality is that not everyone thinks the way you do, otherwise they would have already had the same peculiar idea. You'll need to paint a picture for others and try a variety of means to get your message across. Sometimes you'll need to employ an analogy, a statistic, a historical reference, or maybe even a clever meme, but it is critical to make it real for your audience, so they can imagine the world as you see it.

As a futurist, you will be laughed at, you will be told your ideas are "dumb", and you will be told to get your head out of the clouds (or other places). But you must, despite criticism, persist. This does not mean you should be stubborn or arrogant, but if at the end of a conflict you still believe in your idea, stick with it.

CHAPTER 3:

EAGERNESS TO RALLY AGAINST THE STATUS QUO

A Childhood Change Agent

So what prompts one person to see a new technology and envision the future and another to simply glance over it? What provoked Dave to learn about Bitcoin from his son and see a disruptive force and others to see fool's gold? The desire to question the world around them, "the system", or the status quo seems to be the deciding factor in my opinion. But what does that really mean?

Since I was a child, I have always felt the need to question processes or existing norms,[23] but there are still primary schools teaching cursive when they'd be better off teaching more relevant, practical skills like the basics of computing or Mandarin, so I will admit that challenging the status quo is not always obvious to others.

To dig into this topic, I went to one of my oldest friends and favorite people from childhood Joseph Michael Tasse, Jr., or

---

[23] See my anecdote in the introduction about disputes with my mother about the importance of spelling.

as I typically refer to him, simply "Tasse" – a man whom I've gotten so accustomed to hearing from phrases like "what makes you think that?" and "why is it that people do XYZ when they believe ABC?" that I had to speak with him on questioning the world around us.

Tasse is kind of larger than life. He is a lover of new cultures and languages (particularly those of the romance variety), a Brazilian jiu-jitsu practitioner, a newly minted dual American-Italian citizen, and a maintainer of a bit of a mop of unwieldy hair on his head. The man also has a seemingly unlimited amount of energy and charisma, and I have yet to introduce him to someone and not have them later tell me how much they love the guy. Tasse embraces almost any new opportunities presented his way, is constantly developing new skills, and can make some mean pasta and pastries from scratch (not just the simple stuff either). He and I have also churned through some odds and ends hobbies throughout our childhood[24].

Tasse has extensive experience as both a process optimization consultant and a community organizer. His job experience has literally been spent seeking ways to improve

---

[24] In our early teenage years, we got into making electronic music far before it was mainstream in the way that it is today. His handle was DJ SmoothCoffee and mine was DJ ColdFusion (I know, I know...)

how companies and societies operate. While it would be convenient to focus on the process engineering side of things, this might make for a mundane chapter to the average reader that could be ripped from an industrial operations text on lean manufacturing[25]. Instead, I would like to focus on how Tasse looks at society and questions systems in place that need to change, and perhaps more importantly, how he thinks about influencing others to embrace change[26].

Progress Takes People

As a community organizer for three years with MOSES[27], a non-profit based out of Detroit focused on public transportation, healthcare, civil rights, retail quality, and public safety, Tasse was responsible for understanding the facets of life that were bothering communities in Detroit and how they could fix them by talking to folks about their daily lives. So how does one challenge the status quo by talking to people? Well, it's simple. People will tell you what needs

---

[25] For those more interested – examples of industrial operations improvements would include updating or realigning manufacturing machinery, optimizing inventories, product lines and SKUs (stock keeping units), minimizing transportation times, and getting the right data in the right people's hands at the right time.
[26] Spoiler alert – you can't change an organization or society if you can't inspire and motivate the masses to make a change.
[27] "About Us". *MOSES*. https://mosesmi.org/about-us/ (accessed 15 August 2020).

to be changed if you're just willing to listen and connect with them on an individual level.

According to Tasse, the best way to identify the needs for change is to authentically meet people, and he says he's spent a lifetime devoted to getting new perspectives. From his experience, 95% of people in these communities are just out there trying to survive, so if you walk up to someone with a clipboard and ask, "what is it that you want to change about the current system?", you're probably not going to get a productive answer. You must spend the time to get to know them on a meaningful level.

Diversity of the people you talk to is also important. If you surround yourself by people and experiences that are like yours, it's not going to challenge you much and you're not going to come up with many new ideas, especially those that are going to help their lives. More on this in a couple chapters.

So, what does this have to do with futurism? As a futurist, you are required to see things from a different angle and look for problems that need to be solved, or at the very least the arc of how something today may fill a void tomorrow. Sometimes looking around from one's own vantage point is only so helpful.

Don't get me wrong, I definitely get pissed off every time I need to sign a receipt and will tell anyone I meet how this needs to be replaced by something a bit more digital and/or sophisticated. I mean seriously, why are we still doing this?! But, my personal distaste does not mean enough people feel this way that it is going to go away any time soon unless I can inspire more people to become as unrested by signatures as I do that people in power and influence start to take notice.

At the end of the day, I am just one person, from one part of a corner of this world. Trends don't take place just because I think they urgently need to be changed. If signing receipts pissed everyone off in the same way it does me, they would have been gone years ago. For millennia progress has taken place because society wanted a change, for better or worse. Yet, the change doesn't happen on its own – it takes a person who is able to understand that desire and channel it into a social movement or technological change.

A futurist knows that the world is constantly changing and that nothing remains static unless it remains unquestioned. Questioning is the first step of the journey. If you don't question the world you're in, how could you possibly imagine where it is headed. Tasse questions the social world and system that operates around humanity's daily lives and the operational efficiencies of processes. He does this by understanding people.

Even manufacturing, something one might believe is void of humanity, starts with and is sustained by people. Culture and systems are people. Processes are people. Technology is created and inspired by people. We all know the image (or perhaps the first-hand experience) of a child asking why?" over and over and over and not being satisfied with "it just is".

Be like that.

> **PRINCIPLE #3 – EAGERNESS TO RALLY AGAINST THE STATUS QUO**
> The future does not just happen, it is created by people. It is created because there is a problem to be solved. The role of a futurist is to challenge the world around them and never take "it's the way it is" as an answer. If you think the world will stay the same, just look back on the arc of history and ask, what ever has? And when has it not been driven by a cohesive group of people?

Lifting Up Others

While convenient to think about classical inventors like Thomas Edison, George Westinghouse, and Nikola Tesla challenging the status quo of power generation, not all futurism has to do with high-technology, volts, and genetics. Instead, I would like to talk about the bra. Yes, that bra.

While women had been binding and covering their breasts since the days of ancient Greece, it was not until the early 20th century that a version which somewhat resembles bras of today were created. There is an incredible episode of the show *Drunk History* on this topic, so if you feel like you'll take to this story better told completely hammered by the actress and singer Paget Brewster, skip the next section and pop on Season 3, Episode 11 *"Inventors"* and prepare to laugh[28,29]. If not, proceed.

---

[28] "Inventing the Bra". *Comedy Central*. 10 November 2015. http://www.cc.com/video-clips/w25not/drunk-history-inventing-the-bra (accessed 9 August 2020).

[29] "Inventors". *IMDB*. https://www.imdb.com/title/tt4998722/ (accessed 9 August 2020).

You see in the early 20th century, corsets ruled and constrained women's fashion[30,31], and in 1914, then 19-year-old Mary Phelps Jacobs was on her way to a debutant ball and thought (as Brewster drunkenly narrates during the episode): "Ah, I've got this beautiful silk dress, and I have to put this dumb piece of sh*t on, stupid corset with whale bone inserts, this is so goddamn dumb...I'm out... I'm out... I can't take this". So, she took a couple of handkerchiefs, sewed them together, added some straps and voila![32]

They were an instant success. She knew that every one of her peers hated these things just as much as she did, and she challenged herself to envision a better way. The requests then rolled in from her friends, then strangers, then she was off to the races. She went on to the patent office and after some squabbling ended up with a patent for the backless brassiere. BAM! Adoption was later accelerated by the WWI war effort encouraging women to ditch corsets to save

---

[30] "The First Bra Was Made of Handkerchiefs". *The Atlantic. 3 November 2014.*
https://www.theatlantic.com/technology/archive/2014/11/the-first-bra-was-made-of-handkerchiefs/382283/. (accessed 9 August 2020).
[31] "The History of the Bra". *The Spot by LOLA.*
https://blog.mylola.com/womens-health/history-bra/ (accessed 9 August 2020).
[32] I am certain there was a more sophisticated method to her thought process, but hey, it was 1914, and it's not like there were blogs for her to write everything down in that we can now reference.

metal for weapons, but Mary Phelps Jacobs had the vision to capture what everyone was itching to get rid of and acted (see next chapter for more turning ideas into action).

Creating a Movement

So, what if you yourself are eager to challenge the status quo, but you can't get others to work towards the cause as emphatically because you don't have an idea so universally beloved by peers like the brassiere? If you can't, then you might end up as just one guy or gal on the corner holding up a sign. To make actual systematic change, be it organizational or societal, you need to compel others, and Tasse has developed a honed perspective on this as well.

In our conversation, he described to me how at a certain point in a "call to action" conversation with an individual or group they will agree that a change is necessary but are often unwilling or too afraid to be a part of that change. At that point Tasse says he takes the approach of asking a provoking question or statement that might agitate that individual or group (potentially to the point that they are upset with you) into recognizing that change cannot happen without them. An important caveat to this prescription is that it can only be done effectively if you have taken the time to know and understand the motivations of that individual or group intimately.

Take for instance Tasse's need to convince an undocumented immigrant in Detroit to drive to the state and federal capital, identify themselves as undocumented, and lead a rally cry for immigration reform. Phew! - talk about a scary proposition! At a certain point in their conversation, he says that they came to the fear crossroads – but, as described above, he had taken extensive time to deeply understand her values (primarily religious) and her desire to see her values in action (policy reform).

In order to draw out the awakening that she wasn't living the connection between her values and the outcome she desired to see in the world, he turned to her and said something to the effect of "I think you're afraid to be a leader". As you might imagine, this spurred all sorts of emotions and reactions, and she didn't speak to him for a while, but after they came back to the subject later with calmer minds, she recognized that she needed to be part of the solution and eventually worked up the courage to lead that call for change.

He also made clear that it isn't about just taking a strong position that requires "swagger" or guts to make, you need to show them you're invested in that person or organization and also "show them the way" while empowering them. On more than one occasion Tasse drove her great physical distances, including from Detroit to DC in order to demonstrate that investment and belief in her as well as coaching her on what to do and how to do it. And guess what... after she embraced her ownership in the solution, she convinced others to join the cause as well.

This is very much a simplification of the effort and challenge it took Tasse to influence systematic change but hopefully the gist is clear[33]. Think of it like a good version of a pyramid scheme – you convince three people, they convince three people, and so on, so that by the time you get 10 layers deep you've created about 60,000[34] passionate change agents!

Challenging @ the Office

A few years into my career, a client of mine (that will remain nameless) was going through a major technological

---

[33] Another fun inspiration for gaining a followership and spurring change is by Googling "Leadership Lessons from Dancing Guy" – it's a 3-minute clip that I promise will be worth the watch!

[34] I'll admit I needed a calculator for this one – my mental math, indignance for learning it, and confidence technology would solve the problem was about as strong as it was for spelling.

transformation. They weren't a young start-up hungry to challenge norms, they were (and still are) an aging, behemoth organization over a hundred years old that had succumbed to their own bureaucracy and toxic hierarchical culture.

When my consulting team entered the picture to try to convince them of what might be possible, there was plenty of organizational resistance. Over the century of the company's existence, it had inherited a lot of problematic systems and processes. While the processes were a challenge, the people were even harder. The culture itself was one to shut down those voicing contrary opinions or new ideas that challenged the status quo.

Reprimands would come to those questioning authority and "how things are *just* done". It even went so far as for many employees to visibly display identical posters outside their cubes illustrating the main characters from the animated show *Futurama* in a rehash of an old looking WWII-era poster stating: "YOU'RE NOT PAID TO THINK. A MINDLESS WORKER IS A HAPPY WORKER! SHUT UP AND DO YOUR JOB!"[35]. As you might suspect, the

---

[35] You can even buy them on Amazon: https://amzn.to/3gJkGZm

project was mired with delays, budget run-ups, and under-delivered results. The clear majority of blame which lay squarely on the organization's cultural shoulders.

A mindset that suppresses challenging the status quo is Kryptonite to the futurist. If something like this becomes the common place at your organization, run, do not walk, to the next company. Or if you're feeling bold, take up arms and follow the described path above to motivate systematic change. At the very least take up a short-position against their stock and make a buck or two[36].

In the futurist world you might get responses like "I don't want to look stupid" or "that's too much of a risk for our company" or "what if we lose money?" Well, maybe sometimes you'll have to get comfortable with either understanding, agitating, investing, and coaching those individuals and groups OR accept yourself as a person who just complains about the need for change without being willing to take on risk and be part of the change.

---

[36] *Disclaimer for the SEC*: Please only consider shorting a stock (or taking any non-de minimis financial position) if the decision is based upon publicly and readily available information.

This chapter is best summarized by my favorite T.S. Eliot quote *"Only those who will risk going too far can possibly find out how far one can go."*[37]

---

[37] Why are quotation sites always so cheesy and poorly sourced? If this isn't the right phrasing or if T.S. Eliot wasn't even the one that said it, I am deeply sorry:
"T.S. Eliot Quotes". *Brainy Quote*.
https://www.brainyquote.com/quotes/t_s_eliot_161678 (accessed 9 August 2020).

(If you see this being displayed at any job site or organization, RUN!)

CHAPTER 4:
TAKE ACTION

An Inspirational Icon

This chapter could have served as an extension of the prior chapters on putting in the work, sharing your ideas, and challenging the status quo, but I'll take a small twist to this and call the next principle of a futurist as "taking action".

If you're just studying and sharing, you might remain stuck in a sort of grassroots, activist pigeon hole[38]. To push an idea into reality or win the minds of the general populace in a big way, you'll need to take the next step. This might be writing a book, developing a web forum, starting a company, joining a company, or investing in someone driving your idea forward, but it is important for progress to be made.

For the purposes of this concept, I want to share a story about someone I do not yet have enough clout with to get a one-on-one interview, but someone who I think cannot be

---

[38] There is absolutely nothing wrong with this by the way – being a dreamer and a local evangelist is an amazing gift to yourself, the world, and the people around you!

overlooked in the lineage of futurists, in particular those demonstrating some serious hustle. Martine Rothblatt.

Martine is a less household name than her male counterparts in the futurist, technologist world, but she is a freaking titan[39]. She founded Sirius XM radio[40], runs half triathlons, kills it on the piano[41], was the highest paid female CEO in 2013[42], has 4 children[43], is at the forefront of attempting to digitize the human experience[44], is a UCLA JD/MBA[45] (my

---

[39] Titan (noun), a person of exceptional importance and reputation. Synonyms: behemoth, colossus, giant, heavyweight. Type of: important person, influential person, personage, a person whose actions and opinions strongly influence the course of events.
https://www.vocabulary.com/dictionary/titan (accessed 9 August 2020).
[40] "#65 Martine Rothblatt". *Forbes*. 3 June 2019.
https://www.forbes.com/profile/martine-rothblatt/#30bf24f4c6c0 (accessed 9 August 2020).
[41] "Martine Rothblatt: She founded SiriusXM, a religion and a biotech. For starters." *Washington Post*. 12 December 2014.
https://www.washingtonpost.com/lifestyle/magazine/martine-rothblatt-she-founded-siriusxm-a-religion-and-a-biotech-for-starters/2014/12/11/5a8a4866-71ab-11e4-ad12-3734c461eab6_story.html (accessed 9 August 2020).
[42] "Highest-paid female executive seeks immortality—digitally." *Fortune*. 12 September 2014". https://fortune.com/2014/09/12/highest-paid-female-executive-seeks-immortality-digitally/ (accessed 9 August 2020).
[43] Wikipedia still works:
https://en.wikipedia.org/wiki/Martine_Rothblatt (accessed 9 August 2020).
[44] "Bina Custom Character Robot". *Hanson Robotics*.
https://www.hansonrobotics.com/bina48-9/ (accessed 9 August 2020).
[45] Also Wikipedia: https://en.wikipedia.org/wiki/Martine_Rothblatt (accessed 9 August 2020).

alma mater), has an excellent TED Talk[46], and designed the first production grade electric helicopter (that she can also fly)[47]. Remember what I said about footnotes...[48]

I had the pleasure of hearing Martine speak during my first year at UCLA's MBA program, and it was truly a transformative experience. I remember listening and looking around the room for validation to the question ringing in my head: "is this person for real?!" I will attempt to do her story justice in the following paragraphs, but I highly encourage anyone reading to do some deep dive research on her, because she is about as good as it gets regarding the topic at hand.

Following a Vision Takes Work

In between stints of college in the 70s, Martine had an epiphany while at a NASA tracking station in the Seychelles (talk about hobbies) to unite the world through satellite

---

[46] "Martine Rothblatt: My daughter, my wife, our robot, and the quest for immortality". *TED.* 18 May 2015.
https://www.youtube.com/watch?v=rTJpJlVkRTA (accessed 9 August 2020).
[47] "Martine Rothblatt Creates First Full Size Electric Helicopter". *enrg.io.* 1 November 2016. https://enrg.io/rothblatt-first-full-size-electric-helicopter/ (accessed 9 August 2020).
[48] I said they lend credibility to the speaker or author while saving a lot of time and space.

communications. She decided to go back to college and pursue her undergraduate degree in communications with a thesis on satellite communication. She also engaged with organizations focused on space colonization and went on to pursue her JD/MBA where she published multiple articles on the law of satellite communications and prepared a plan for how to bring satellite technology to Latin American countries. She was then retained by the founder of a Spanish speaking television network to implement her plan. After falling at odds with the organization, she founded Sirius Satellite radio in 1990[49]. We've all likely heard of this organization and what it did to disrupt an entire industry, so I won't belabor this point.

While I attempted to summarize 20+ years' worth of effort in a single paragraph, Martine took action! Year after year, hour after hour, Martine focused on building the research, credentials, and passion to put forth a transformative idea – never giving up until it was fulfilled. Martine isn't just a smooth salesperson (although she is), she is incredibly driven and hardworking. If the story on Martine ended here,

---

[49] Seriously, how great is Wikipedia: https://en.wikipedia.org/wiki/Martine_Rothblatt (accessed 9 August 2020).

it would be a fantastic, in-and-out story about hustling to bring a futurist idea to life. But this is just the start.

Martine is someone who sees problems in the world and is compelled to address them. She is the type of futurist that doesn't just sit at a keyboard on forums pontificating (I'll awkwardly admit to being one of those at times) – she goes out and acts. So, when her daughter was diagnosed with a rare, life-threatening form of pulmonary hypertension in 1994 – she had to do something.

> **PRINCIPLE #4 – TAKE ACTION**
> If you are just sitting behind a keyboard putting thoughtware out on the internet and telling your friends your wild ideas – that is likely where your idea will land. Grassroots activism is important, and the baby steps needed to push an idea forward, but to really make the future a reality, you must have skin in the game and get after it. Write a book, apply to give a TED talk, change careers, make an investment, or anything to push your agenda to the next level!

Activist Futurism

So, what does any normal person do when their child faces such an adversity as Martine? Naturally, you identify a company leading research in the field, acquire it, and found a biopharma company to find a treatment. United Therapeutics became the name of the company, and in 2002, the FDA approved its treatment for the disorder, Remodulin[50] and her daughter remains alive and well to this day. From there she continued to pioneer improvements within the pulmonary field for years to come and remains the CEO of the company to this day. Wow, right...

So, what about the courage part of the equation from the previous chapters? She clearly has the hustle, willingness to take action, and probably some natural gift[51]. So, where is the courage and persistence that is so critical to a compelling

---

[50] Herper, Matthew. "From Satellites to Pharmaceuticals". Forbes. April 22, 2010. https://www.forbes.com/forbes/2010/0510/second-acts-pharmaceuticals-orphan-drugs-pah-deep-breaths.html#1ff3d39d597a. (accessed 9 August 2020).

[51] I generally shirk at the notion of giftedness since it tends to serve as an excuse for those who don't view themselves that way – as I'll argue in this book, you can become a futurist, musician, or an author if you're willing to put in the effort. I do think some folks have a head start or a disproportionate chance to achieve top-tier success though. Michael Phelps is a genetic freak of nature that I would never be able to beat no matter how much I practiced if he too trained as he does. But, with enough effort – I could probably beat Phelps if he had never put in the effort to train.

futurist you ask? Well for starters, around the time she founded United Therapeutics, she came out as transgender. In both the predominantly "good ole boys" clubs that are telecom and big pharma, that takes a ton of guts or as Tasse would say "swagger". Sharing the outlandish ideas Martine is famous for with a global community who once knew you as a man but now as a woman… well, if she can do that, you can tell your boss at work about a new idea to streamline the company or your parents that you want to go to space camp!

Getting Bored is a Good Thing

I am convinced that Martine Rothblatt must get bored very easily, which I think is a nice foundation for a futurist. As if founding Sirius Radio and United Therapeutics was not enough, she continues to push the frontier of Artificial Intelligence (Google search "BINA48"), cyber-consciousness, electric helicopters[52], sustainable building, and social activism regarding transgender rights[53].

On the topic of the electric helicopters – it is important to note that like Elon Musk catching flak for a mass production electric vehicle being nothing but a pipe dream, Martine also

---

[52] She currently maintains the Guinness Book record for longest electric flight.
[53] See previous footnotes – seriously though, read those links.

was criticized for her idea being impossible, so once again, courage (and maybe some capital to burn) is always going to be important in this game. More on claims of impossibility later.

CHAPTER 5:
HAVE FUN WITH IT

Mr. Smith Goes to the Web

I met Michael Kleinmann during the mid-point of my consulting career while on a project based in the Southeastern United States. He was leading an engagement at a healthcare organization, and our team was tasked with analyzing the potential impact of technology on their patients and services. They wanted to envision how healthcare may be impacted by technology on a time horizon of the decades instead of the one to five-year strategic work most clients requested. It was a project that really galvanized my desire to make a profession out of futurism, and I would not have had this realization without Michael.

Michael's professional foyer into science and technology was less anointed by birth as it was with Dave, but nevertheless tells a good story. Michael originally started his career running political campaigns in the 90s until one year he was supporting a State Assemblyman in Wisconsin who was co-chair of the Joint Committee on Information Policy and Technology, which included interpretation of the

Telecommunications Act of 1996[54] for the State of Wisconsin. Through this work, that happened to coincide with the early commercialization of the Internet, Michael realized there was a disruptive technology force emerging and joined a consulting firm known for projects with the United States government – leading to work supporting early federal applications of the Internet.

It was at this point that Michael had a similar "protracted aha" as Dave described where he realized that the Internet was going to change humanity. He went on to launch a series of Internet-based companies that were well ahead of their time including a particularly unique project with the intent to tap into the wisdom of retirees remotely to assist in assorted projects for startups and small businesses so that their accumulated knowledge would not be lost simply because they were no longer active in the traditional workforce. Pretty awesome stuff, right? While it did not ultimately take off, it was a genuinely innovative way of

---

[54] The Telecommunications Act of 1996 was the first significant overhaul of telecommunications law in more than sixty years, amending the Communications Act of 1934. The Act, signed by President Bill Clinton, represented a major change in American telecommunication law, since it was the first time that the Internet was included in broadcasting and spectrum allotment.
"The Telecommunications Act of 1996. Title 3, sec. 301." *FCC.* https://transition.fcc.gov/Reports/tcom1996.pdf. (accessed 9 August 2020).

thinking about the early Internet and communications technologies.

An Entertaining Visionary

A fellow Midwesterner from Milwaukee, Michael is a very paternal person to work with. While you're on his team (and after) he genuinely cares about you. Not just your career progression and development, but your personal passions, interests, and what makes you tick.

Due to the general Monday through Thursday travel of the management consulting world[55], Michael and I had plenty of time to get to know each other while on the road sharing breakfast, lunch, and dinner daily. Rather than superficial table talk about sports or the weather, Michael relishes in seeding discussions with philosophical or theoretical

---

[55] The standard operating procedure of "consulting" is that you and your team fly from whatever city you live in to wherever your client is no matter how far on Monday morning and then return Thursday evening back to wherever you live. I've been based out of Los Angeles and Detroit but have had work in Puerto Rico, Miami, Cape Cod, Eastern Maine, Hong Kong, Seattle, Pittsburgh, random towns in Indiana and Ohio you've likely never heard of, and everywhere in between. You rinse and repeat this process week after week until the project is complete, and there is little expectation of weeks working remotely throughout (although this may change in the post-COVID era). It can be a tiresome grind, but you do rack up a ton of hotel points, flight miles, and statuses that only other consultants seem to care about and most of your friends just roll their eyes at.

questions to dig into a line of thinking that is a bit more challenging. After all, Michael was the first person to introduce me to the idea of quantum computing – a concept that when thought about heavily still tends to melt my brain a bit[56].

During a team dinner, he asked the table if we could go back in time and change one event, what would it be? I had already thought of this one before and indicated I would stop the fire which destroyed the Library of Alexandria in the first century BC. It was said to have contained all the knowledge of humanity at the time, and its destruction is thought to have set back scientific and technological progress 500 years[57]. If it hadn't burned down, we'd probably be in flying cars by now. My answer wasn't the classic response of "kill Hitler" and was exactly the scenario that Michael said he too would prevent from happening. It was a clear indicator to both of us that we were wired the same (maybe strange) way.

---

[56] Mandelbaum, Ryan. "What the Hell Is a Quantum Computer and How Excited Should I Be?" *Gizmodo*. 11 July 2017. https://gizmodo.com/what-the-hell-is-a-quantum-computer-and-how-excited-sho-1819296509. (accessed 9 August 2020).
[57] Crawford, James. "The Life and Death of the Library of Alexandria". *LitHub*. 13 March 2017. https://lithub.com/the-life-and-death-of-the-library-of-alexandria/. (accessed 9 August 2020).

Since then, Michael and I have spent many a late night over food and beverage pontificating about the future. We've talked through the concept of a "digital twin" which simulates in the digital world permutations of what your life could be and advises you on the actions to take. We've conceptualized a world where each person owns and controls their personal data, including health, geolocation, and consumption patterns and possess the ability to sell their data to the highest bidding company rather than the non-monetizing, data leeching of today. We've even talked about the failed human-ape hybrid experiments of the 1920s[58] and how such efforts are rumored to being re-explored in present day China. Suffice it to say, Michael is an entertaining person to talk with. His light-hearted, conversationalist demeaner fosters this sort of "free space" that allows your brain to drop preconceptions and just go on the journey.

I jokingly call Michael a conspiracy theorist from time to time for some of his wild ideas, but the truth is Michael is anything but, and we both love exploring provocative and outlandish ideas in a way that is somewhat competitive as to

---

[58] Research "humanzees" if you're curious. Or the usual: https://en.wikipedia.org/wiki/Humanzee

who can push the "art of the possible"[59] the farthest. Predicting the future is a ridiculous thing to do sometimes and often calls for a less than serious attitude and quite a bit of laughter.

When children draw something silly like an animal doctor no one bats an eye, but if you talk to the CTO of a major corporation about robotic doctors and selling your health information to the highest bidder, suddenly everyone loses their mind!

> ### PRINCIPLE #5 – HAVE FUN WITH IT
> Being too serious all the time can restrict your imagination, and you'll need a lot of it to be a futurist. Audiences tend not to respond well to a solemn demeanor (see commentary on Dawkins from previous chapter) and are more receptive when they feel like they're having a good time. Plus, who wants to do a job that you can't laugh at a little!

---

[59] "Art of the possible" is a consulting term coined to mean "thinking outside the box", but we can't very well charge people to tell them to "just think creatively".

The Jovial Billionaire

Designing the future does not need to be a serious, stoic business. You can have fun, you can laugh, and you can tap into that child-like disregard for reality that you've long since forgotten. But can this carefree, dreaming yield actual results? Is it a practical approach to running the most efficient organization on the planet? Perhaps not. But, if you want to dream big or evolve your thinking, it can be quite helpful.

The most prominent business leader that comes to mind that embodies this is persona is Richard Branson. Creating his first business at the age of 16, Branson went on to found Virgin Group – a company which today controls over 400 companies across a variety of industries[60]. Among his various ventures (some failures and some wins), my personal favorite is, as a futurist nerd, Virgin Galactic.

In 2004, part in place to compete for an XPRIZE ten-million-dollar prize for the first non-governmental organization to launch a reusable manned spacecraft into suborbital space, Branson sponsored a promising concept "SpaceShipOne" that would go on to successfully obtain the winning purse

---
[60] You guessed it: https://en.wikipedia.org/wiki/Virgin_Group

and shortly thereafter make lofty promises about the future of space tourism[61].

While Virgin Galactic has encountered major operational setbacks and frequent delays, it has remained resilient and opened the first commercial spaceport on Earth in August 2019 and became publicly traded two months later. Despite the ebbs and flows of success with this endeavor, Branson has never lost his upbeat, captivating attitude. Managing to stay above the fray and not to get into billionaire Twitter matches over space superiority that Bezos of Blue Origin and Musk of SpaceX have been dragged into[62] – Branson is almost always seen with a smile and a laugh.

Well before the founding of Virgin Galactic, after pulling a notable public gag in 1999 where he flew a blimp reading "BA CAN'T GET IT UP!" to poke fun at their competitor, British Airways (BA), Branson told an audience "Being a bit cheeky and having a bit of fun is good – not taking yourself too seriously is important." This mentality persists today. In fact, if you navigate to the page within Virgin's website that

---

[61] "SpaceShipOne rockets to success". *BBC News.* 7 October 2005. http://news.bbc.co.uk/2/hi/science/nature/3712998.stm. (accessed 9 August 2020).

[62] "Elon Musk Just Trolled Jeff Bezos on Twitter and It Could Reignite a Years-Old Feud Between the Billionaires". *Entrepreneur.* 10 April 2019. https://www.entrepreneur.com/article/332036

discusses Branson, you are met with a banner that reads "Don't take yourself seriously, no one else does[63]."

In 2005, I remember quite vividly as a teenager watching an *MTV Cribs* episode where Branson himself shows the crew around his recently purchased Necker Island estate wearing a head to toe white canvas outfit with a very, *very* deep-V neckline. He laughs and gestures as he leisurely strolls across the island[64]. With my educational eyes on entering college and pursuing a degree in business, I thought to myself: "this is not the mentality of a banker, grounded in numbers and statistics, focused on rules of economics and pushing the envelope of financial regulations. This is a dreamer."

Balance in All Things

During my conversation with Michael, we analyzed this mentality a bit further. Is a humorous perspective more effective than one anchored in seriousness? We came to a

---

[63] "Don't take yourself too seriously, nobody else does". *Virgin.* https://www.virgin.com/richard-branson/dont-take-yourself-too-seriously-nobody-else-does. (accessed 9 August 2020).
[64] "Cribs around the world". *MTV.* http://www.mtv.com/video-clips/ru0odn/mtv-cribs-cribs-around-the-world. (accessed 9 August 2020).

common consultant answer: "It depends."[65] A good futurist is not necessarily stoic and snippy. You aren't going to attract or draw people into your ideas with black and white video and bleak depictions of the future, you'll need to employ a bit of humor, optimism, and a great deal of imagination. Even once serious individuals such as Elon Musk have with increasing regularity taken to Twitter (he should honestly pump the breaks here a bit) with the occasional joke, or meme, or launching an actual flamethrower product from time to time.

There does, however, seem to be a balance between the creative/free-spiritedness and the productive/organized that is necessary to bring to light new ideas. Swing too far into the clouds and you'll never move from the back of a napkin to a prototype. Go too far to the practical, and you'll never make changes beyond the incremental.

Enter my personal favorite consulting tool, the 2 x 2 matrix! If you plot the personality style of the individual on the X-axis and their orientation to detail on the Y-axis, you get a handy framework for how to view futurist archetypes:

---

[65] We seriously say this a ton in the business – it buys us some time while we think about a better answer.

FUTURST ARCHETYPE FRAMEWORK

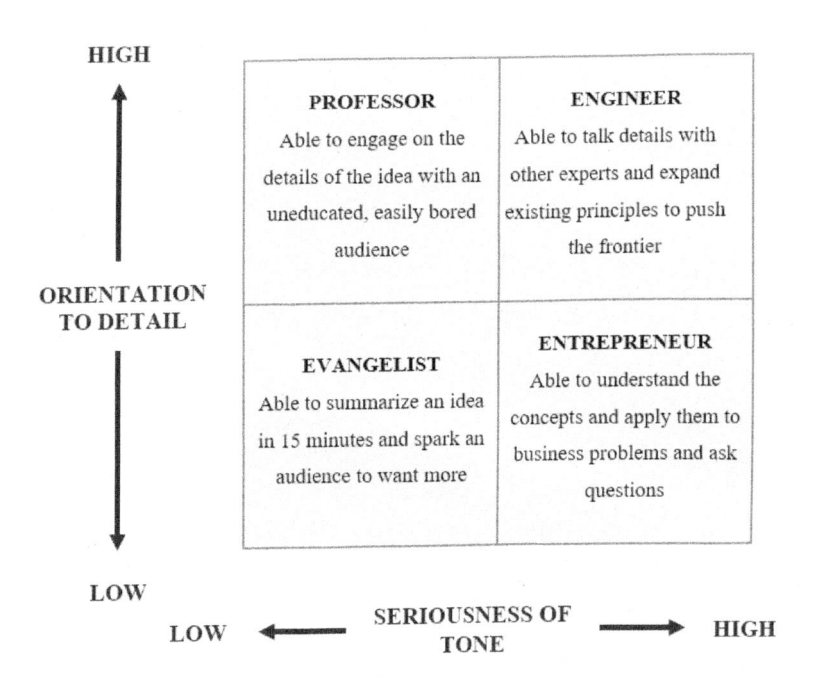

HIGH ↑ **ORIENTATION TO DETAIL** ↓ **LOW**	**PROFESSOR** Able to engage on the details of the idea with an uneducated, easily bored audience	**ENGINEER** Able to talk details with other experts and expand existing principles to push the frontier
	EVANGELIST Able to summarize an idea in 15 minutes and spark an audience to want more	**ENTREPRENEUR** Able to understand the concepts and apply them to business problems and ask questions

LOW ← **SERIOUSNESS OF TONE** → HIGH

As depicted above, each combination of tone and detail results in a different outcome and effect:

- **Professor** – The futurist who can talk and train others for hours upon hours on a topic without becoming boring (ideally); employs fresh perspectives and engages the audience in exercises to ground the concept and improve upon it.
- **Evangelist** – The futurist on stage giving the TED Talk; Able to speak succinctly and entertainingly about the concept and get the audience to leave with a nugget of an idea that might make them come back for more.
- **Engineer** – The futurist that is truly "pushing the science" behind the idea whether it be in web forums or skunk works, the engineer is responsible for figuring out the incremental steps needed to draw the path ahead for the idea.
- **Entrepreneur** – the futurist that turns an idea into a business and explains the value of the idea on the future of an organization; the founders, Chief Technology, Strategy, or Digital Officers of the world.

Each of the above descriptions are unique in and of themselves and very few people can jump between them all (save Musk, Jobs, and a handful of others), but each provide great value and can be equally "futurist" by design[66]. To drive forward a far-out concept, you need all these people on your team. No one can be all things, so figure out which style aligns best with you and focus on developing a persona to match, and then go find the other individuals to fill in the gaps. More on building a team later.

---

[66] IMHO

CHAPTER 6: FOSTER CREATIVITY

Creative Practicality

As mentioned in the previous chapter, it is difficult to keep the light-hearted nature of futurism in balance with the serious "listen to what I have to say" side of the house. I have also found, by working through challenging client problems, that it can be equally difficult to create a balanced tension between the creative and the practical.

If you keep an idea abstract and dreamy, it can often be too intangible for anyone to grab ahold of, or imagine it applied to their life or the organization they are a part of. But distilling an idea into a prescriptive product complete with dimensionality, shape, color, and discrete capabilities leaves little room for the brain to explore areas to expand from or adjust the idea.

CREATIVITY-PRACTICALITY CONTINUUM

| Too Practical / Concrete | ←——————●——————→ *The Futurist Sweet Spot* | Too Creative / Abstract |

Training the brain to balance these two worlds is a challenge, but not impossible. My friend and former colleague, Jon Gilchrist, is one of those individuals who has managed such a feat and can jump into different mindsets so well that he believes there are multiple "instances" of himself: the artist, the technologist, the emotionally exposed, and friendship embracing. Suffice it to say, Jon is a complex and deep individual. But he was not born this way, he helped shaped himself over time.

Jon was among the first people I worked with when I returned from grad school and was stationed on a project in Albuquerque, New Mexico. It was only a 10-week project, but as noted in my section on Michael Kleinmann, the management consulting world can bring people together quickly. Jon and I have since worked across the country together in New England, Detroit, Kentucky, and Seattle within the healthcare world we had both focused on at the time.

Jon's current professional area of specialty centers around mergers and acquisitions, operational efficiencies, and technology roadmaps – work that would classically be described as left brain, logical thinking. Yet, Jon can also be an incredibly right-brained, creative thinker[67]. When we first began working together, he and I often had obscure conversations (perhaps not as wild as my conversations with Michael, but nevertheless engaging).

After his mother passed several years ago, he began exploring more about her life. Unbeknownst to him until her death, she was a painter for much of her life, and he believes that part of her creative energy at that time was passed on to him. And so began Jon's journey into art. Without formal training or background, he bought a few canvases, the minimum brushes and tools and jumped right in.

If this were a Hollywood movie, this is where Jon's first touch of paint to canvas resulted in an engaging, abstract portrait of his mother that captures the attention of an esteemed art agent and suddenly he's featured in a prestigious art gallery in Zurich. But that is not how this story goes or the real world works.

---

[67] Everything I've read recently from a science perspective says that the left-right brain analogy is a fallacy, but it still makes for good shorthand.

Consultant-Painter / Painter-Consultant

Jon has a solid build, shaved head, and always well-tailored clothing on, usually accompanied by a few standout accessories. A pocket square, novelty cufflinks, or a bold-colored strapped watch are a mainstay of Jon's attire at work[68]. He also has an incredibly bellowing laugh that can't help but warm you up. Jon is the kind of guy that walks into a room and you can feel the comfortability inside him. Jon is also incredibly fearless. And, it is with this fearlessness that Jon chronicled his journey into art on social media. He wasn't in it for the likes or the retweets. But as an artist, he wanted his work to be experienced.

Jon focuses primarily on abstract art, and his first set of paintings were a little rough. There was certainly nothing wrong with them, as art IS in the eye of the beholder. They were much better than I could do, but they weren't anything to move you to grab your phone, show the person next to you, and say "hey, look what this guy I know is doing". But that is entirely the point of developing a skill. No master violinist ever picked up an instrument and perfectly

---

[68] His work place aesthetic is something I mimicked the more we worked together, and he served as a professional attire benchmark for if I was properly assembled in any given day.

performed Vivaldi's Concerto no. 2 in E minor on their initial go.

Jon vividly recalls the first time that he showcased an art piece. It was in January 2017 at an event in Houston called *"Pancakes and Booze"*. He had progressed quite a bit in his art and was rather proud of what he had put on the canvas as it was displayed in front of onlookers grabbing their food. Standing on stage observing the procession of people, Jon saw a group of three men observing his piece. One of them made a sour face and tapped his buddy on the shoulder. They too looked and made an equally unpleasant face. As Jon describes his art: "it is physically a piece of me on the canvas" – and that sort of reception hurt.

While Jon was crushed by it, he did not allow it to break him. When embarking on this creative journey, Jon swore that he wasn't going to let social acceptance dictate how he felt about his art. But it did get him to double his resolve. Jon insists that you can't grow by staying in your comfort zone. He says that he learned this at a young age being the only black man in a room and needing to be comfortable and confident. From there he has always pushed himself through a wide variety of challenges. Shark diving, yoga, triathlons, sports cars, coffee, and world travel are just a few of Jon's varied passions. So, between spurts of artistic pursuits, Jon has outside passions to separate himself from his art entirely – and the science behind creativity says that this is how it's meant to be.

How Creativity Works

In the 2012 book *Imagine: How Creativity Works*, Jonah Lehrer outlines how creativity scientifically works, predominantly using historic technological and business events[69,70]. One aspect of this work includes how creativity is derived from focusing heavily on the task at hand (in Jon's case art, in our case futurism), stepping away from the task to do something completely unrelated, and then getting back into your creative work.

Creativity takes place when your brain draws upon varied experiences, creates new connections, and then over time you get the famous "aha!" moment or in the case of Dave

---

[69] It's a good read worth purchasing:
Lehrer, Jonah. "Imagine: How Creativity Works". *Houghton Mifflin.* 1 January 2012.
https://www.amazon.com/Imagine-Creativity-Works-Jonah-Lehrer/dp/B007QRI1UQ (accessed 9 August 2020).
[70] If you don't want to buy and read the book, here is a good summary: "#12. A Summary of 'Imagine: How Creativity Works' by Jonah Lehrer" *New Books in Brief.* 29 April 2012.
"http://newbooksinbrief.com/2012/04/29/12-a-summary-of-imagine-how-creativity-works-by-jonah-lehrer/ (accessed 9 August 2020).

and Bitcoin, a "protracted aha!". Put simply, the more random things you cram into your brain, the more novel pathways that are created and the greater likelihood you are struck with a genuinely new idea.

This kind Perspiration-Inspiration-Perspiration pattern famously took place in the late 60s with the invention of the sticky note. At the time, A chemist at 3M was on the quest to develop an ultra-strong adhesive and accidentally developed a low-tack adhesive. It was a product that served no discernable purpose given his directive to develop the complete opposite outcome. 3M was notorious during this era for sharing ideas with people across the company outside of the design team assigned to the product, and for five years, various groups were exposed to the adhesive without avail.

One day, one of those people exposed to the adhesive was singing in his church choir and was frustrated that bookmarks kept falling out of the hymnal books. He then thought of the minimally adhesive substance he had been exposed to and ta-da!, it worked perfectly! The famous *Post-it Note* was launch soon thereafter. However, it was not an initial success. It took several more years of iterative improvement in marketing, product, and packaging for it to become a success in the 80s.[71] Nevertheless, had the low-tack adhesive not been presented to such an array of people, we might not have such an iconic product in almost all our desk drawers.

Give Yourself Permission to be Creative

In a June 2020 TED Talk from the actor Ethan Hawke titled *"Give yourself permission to be creative"*, he argues... well exactly that, give yourself permission to be creative!

> *"The pull of habit is so huge, and that's what makes kids so beautifully creative – they don't have any habits, and they don't care if they're any good – they're not building a sand castle going 'I think I'm going to be a real good sand castle builder' – they just throw themselves at whatever project you put in front of them: dancing, doing a painting, you know, building something, any opportunity they have they try to use it to impress upon you their individuality"*

---

[71] "History Timeline: Post-it® Notes". *Post-it.com.* https://www.post-it.com/3M/en_US/post-it/contact-us/about-us/. (accessed 9 August 2020).

Rather than talk too much else about it because I can't do it justice like he can, just go Google it. It's free online[72].

> **PRINCIPLE #6 – FOSTER CREATIVITY**
>
> Futurism exists predominantly in the world of creativity. However, creativity is not something you are primarily either born with or not. Most children can conjure up the fantastical with relative ease, but then somewhere along the way it is lost. Creativity is hard work, and you need to put in the effort to keep your creativity sharp in order to combine practical worldly experience with child-like musings.

---

[72] "Give yourself permission to be creative". *TED*. June 2020. https://www.ted.com/talks/ethan_hawke_give_yourself_permission_to_be_creative?language=en. (accessed 9 August 2020).

Fall in Love with Being a Generalist

One of the keys to fostering the kind of creativity required to become a futurist is to create novel neural connections. In the same way 3M exposed employees to concepts outside of their field and projects, you must expose yourself to novelty and let your brain draw out the connections. This will mean stepping outside of your comfort area and pushing yourself into new arenas as Jon does. You may say to yourself, I love art already though, I am a creative person. But classical creativity in the arts is not enough. Constantly exposing yourself to art is just strengthening a small specified area of your brain devoted to conventional art.

Perhaps you've always judged people who are into NASCAR. You should go to a race. Maybe you feel most comfortable taking beach vacations. It's probably time to strap on a backpack and trek around Southeast Asia. Or maybe you really love videogames, and it's time to start training for that half marathon. Live mostly in the digital world? Time to buy some acrylics, some canvases, brushes, a nice tarp and get after it! Think anime is lame? Well, over a billion people across the world watch it, so maybe give it a shot[73].

The point here is that your brain can only make wild associations when you give it something novel to connect with. I've heard some communities online call this concept "idea sex[74]", in that you're mating two separate ideas with each other, but I'll just call it "drawing unique connections". You'll learn a new skillset or experience and at the same time "free your mind"[75] to imagine what the future may look like.

Once again, science seems to back this idea up. In a 20-year study of 284 professional forecasters, analysis of over 80,000 forecasts showed that experts are less accurate predictors than non-experts in their area of specialty. A *Harvard Business Review* article on the study concluded that "ideological reliance on a single perspective appears detrimental to one's ability to successfully navigate vague or poorly-defined situations[76]".

---

[73] *Samurai Champloo, Full Metal Alchemist: Brotherhood, Cowboy Bebop, Attack on Titan*, and *My Hero Academia* are palatable starts.
[74] "What is Idea Sex?" *The Week.* 10 August 2010. https://theweek.com/articles/492012/what-idea-sex. (accessed 9 August 2020).
[75] Again, with *The Matrix* references
[76] Mansharamani, Vikram. "All Hail the Generalist". *Harvard Business Review.* 4 June 2012. https://hbr.org/2012/06/all-hail-the-generalist. (accessed 9 August 2020).

Generalism in Action

Within the consulting world, I had been quite a bit of a generalist. I recently inventoried the arc of my consulting career, and my work has almost always centered around technology. I also found that during a decade, I've worked at 25 different organizations ranging in size from a 20-person non-profit organization to publicly traded companies in with tens of thousands of employees. Some projects were less than one month long; some lasted well over a year. Many were in major metropolitan areas – others were in towns with less than 20,000 residents. I've operated in the Pacific Northwest, the Midwest, the East Coast, Hong Kong, Ethiopia, and the Caribbean. I've spent time in healthcare, oil and gas, retail, consumer goods, manufacturing, non-profits/government, and media/entertainment. I've worked on mergers and acquisitions, data analytics implementations, disruptive technology scans, cost reduction efforts, and enterprise roadmaps. Perhaps the most consistent theme from my career has been inconsistency.

While at times being a generalist has been a challenge when a project wanted someone deep in expertise on say cloud computing, I was generally sought after on broader-thinking projects due to my flexibility and way of pulling from different experiences to come up with a novel idea or outcome. The number of times I drew upon a different industry or type of work than the current engagement to inspire a decision were too many to count. Had I gone deep on a single topic, there is no way I could have come to any number of realizations.

When Michael Kleinmann and I spoke about futurism, we talked at length about how diverse the interests and pursuits were of some of the Renaissance inventors – so much that the term "renaissance man or woman" has become established in common vocabulary to this day. If you look at Leonardo da Vinci's Wikipedia page, it states that he is "Known for painting, drawing, sculpting, science, engineering, architecture, anatomy". Based on what we've covered thus far, it is no surprise that often the most brilliant inventors, futurists, and creators are known for such a wide aperture of pursuits. The building of new neural pathways across broad topics creates new and exciting ideas!

In my work, needing to catch up on an entire industry over a weekend or lead a team on a subject matter I was unfamiliar with had always been stressful though. Almost without fail, on each new project, I would confide in someone close to me with something along the lines of: "you don't understand –

this is the time I may be out of my depth here…people are going to find out that I'm a fraud!" These confidants who knew me and my pattern of thought would reply with: "Adam – you say this every time, you will be fine".

This imposter syndrome would proceed for a couple weeks, and then suddenly I would report to them "hey – I figured it out and we're delivering really great work out here!" It is this process of angst followed by growth in order to drive creativity that never quite went away, although I did learn to accept it when it appeared and greet it like an old friend. Now when I encounter something professionally or personally unfamiliar, I try to say to myself "Oh. hello anxiety monster, it's been a while…"

The fear associated with growth experiences required to drive creative thought is just a part of life, whether it is consulting, painting, or bobsledding….

Get Comfortable with Being Uncomfortable

During my consulting career, one of the companies I worked for were major sponsors of the Olympics. As such, they often had medaling athletes on call to speak at events. During a week-long consulting boot camp, our closing speaker was Steve Mesler. In his talk, he told the journey he took as a professional athlete and the angst confrontation required for growth[77].

In high school and college, he was a track star, but every season he would blow out his leg and need to be benched for a part of the year. Year after year, the cycle would repeat until someone pulled him aside and gave him "the talk". First, they gave him the bad news. Perhaps track was not meant for him. The good news, they were quite confident that he would succeed as a bobsledder. Similar use of leg muscles and endurance but not in a way that would continue to damage his injury.

He was skeptical. He had always felt so comfortable being a track athlete. After some persistence, he decided to give it a shot. His first time down the track he described was jarring. Apparently, you get banged around, it's loud, and it hurts. The next time down, a little bit better. The next even more comfortable. Until one day, you're excited by your progress, and you become exhilarated by the experience. In

---

[77] He is also apparently a pretty nice guy:
Kolur, Nihal. "Olympic Bobsledder Steve Mesler Spreads his Message to Kids Through Classroom Champions". *Sports Illustrated.* 20 November 2017. https://www.si.com/olympics/2017/11/20/olympics-bobsled-steve-mesler-classroom-champions. (accessed 9 August 2020).

2010, Steve's four-man bobsled team won the gold medal at the Vancouver Olympics.

Speaking more broadly about the challenge of growth opportunities, Steve said (as best I can recall) "you have to get comfortable with being uncomfortable, in order to get comfortable." His point being that almost nothing "comes naturally". You don't hop into a bobsled, stand up in front of your first 100-person audience, pick up a paintbrush, or put down your first futurist theory and think "well that felt perfect!". The same speaks for the type of experiences that will create new pathways for creativity. Experiences that you think will be uncomfortable are those that you need to think to yourself "I am nervous about this, which means I need to do this".

An Unfinished Journey

So, did Jon ever "get good" at art? Well he's been at it almost every week for 3 years now, and while he strongly believes his journey is never over, he has made incredible progress. From paintings that once evoked my response of "well, that is nice that he has a hobby" to "that would really fit well on my wall – how much does it cost?" in a relatively short-time is impressive.

From being made to feel small during a local art venue to being featured at *Art Basel* in Miami in December 2019 (a premier venue for any artist) is somewhat of a dream come true for Jon. But it has been hard work. Jon is constantly practicing his craft, exposing himself to other inspirational art, and participating in an array of disparate activities that can help foster a creative spark.

(Jon with two of his pieces at Art Basel Miami 2019)

As a futurist, you cannot afford to simply seek inspiration from traditional futuristic sources such as science fiction movies[78]; you must push yourself outside of your comfort zone and expose yourself to new ideas and activities that

---

[78] I do love science fiction though and recently completed a ranking of my top 150 science fiction movies of all time. Message me, and I'll pass along my list.

challenge your stabled state of mind and perspective. You must also put in the same level of effort Dave put into Bitcoin into every endeavor you explore.

Spend time mulling the idea, doing research, reviewing your concept with peers, and continuously breaking apart and rebuilding your concept – but also step away to pick up an entirely different skill or hobby. While there are examples of Epiphanius discoveries, the reality is that those epiphanies typically occur after countless hours of failures (and likely time between work to explore other avenues).

At the end of the day, fostering a creative mindset is not free, it comes at a cost. To truly hone the skill, you must be willing to put in the sweat equity and put yourself in the best position for the "aha!" moment. Becoming creative is just as challenging as learning a new coding or spoken language, so if you're simply waiting around for an inspiration, you might be waiting a long time. Seek out opportunities to push through discomfort, build new neural connections, and channel the creative burst that follows!

CHAPTER 7:
FIND A PARTNER

The Lonely Futurist

A common thread I encountered in speaking with individuals for this book is that it can, at times, be difficult to find others who like to intellectually spar about the future. The majority of my conversations for this book ended with an exchange encouraging one another to reach out if they wanted to hash out a wild concept or talk about a radical idea in science or technology news.

This was a bit of a surprise to me because I can almost never shut up about it and tend to steer almost any conversation from shoes to food in that direction at any opportunity. But upon reflection, I too only have a handful of people who will tolerate my line of rambling for more than the obligatory minute or two before steering the conversation to something more relevant or practical.

This can be a challenge to developing a futurist concept as there is historical evidence that working with others on creative, intellectual endeavors can be quite beneficial. As a history buff, Michael Kleinmann weighed in on this one as well. Ever since the days of Plato, ideas have been publicly workshopped, debated, and refined time and time again. During the 15th – 17th centuries, coffeehouses[79] were an enormous source of intellectual socialization and debate. There were also the salons of the 18th and 19th centuries[80] which provided similar purposes and then universities thereafter. Time and time again patterns emerge of thought exchange strengthening and evolving ideas.

Now we have the Internet. While this is an incredible tool that has resulted in the spread of the volume of information, it has led to a bit of a degradation in quality and the ability to have a real-time exchange that is hard to be replaced via anonymous web forums and other communities. Surely this will continue to improve as more immersive experiences such as virtual reality (VR) and augmented reality (AR) continue to evolve, but for now it can be a bit of a cluster driven by anonymity and the more than occasional troll hell-bent on spreading misinformation and undermining progress

---

[79] "How Café Culture Helped Make Good Ideas Happen". *NPR.* 17 October 2010.
https://www.npr.org/templates/story/story.php?storyId=130595037. (accessed 9 August 2020).
[80] "The Salons". *Alpha History.*
https://alphahistory.com/frenchrevolution/salons/. (accessed 9 August 2020).

"for the lolz"[81]. So, the Internet can be a bit of a minefield, but it can be a nice place to start. After all, Bitcoin was developed by a group of anonymous weirdos on a web forum and as of April 2021 over $1 trillion is being held in the currency.

Whether it is the internet, a university, or through your personal or professional network, you must actively seek out partners – people who can debate and push back on your idea and perhaps bring his or her own spin on the concept.

> **PRINCIPLE #7 – FIND A PARTNER**
> Without someone to talk to, being a futurist is a very isolating experience. Not only that, a lack of dialogue will limit the bounds of your idea. In order to be successful, you need a team (or just a patient friend) to help breakdown and re-build your ideas.

---

[81] Also known as "for sh*ts and giggles"

The Benefit of Abrasion

In either school or work, someone introduced me to the term "cultural abrasion" that I think speaks incredibly well to this topic. The idea is that individuals with different backgrounds (i.e., gender, ethnicity, age, orientation, geography, politics) provide unique perspectives that help drive better outcomes in almost anything intellectual, professional, or creative.

By surrounding oneself with individuals of similar backgrounds, in a sense we are working with yes men or women and will only, on average, get perspective within a couple degrees of separation from ourselves. When I heard the term, it was used to advocate greater diversity within companies to bring out more complete solutions and ideas, but it rings true for fleshing out a futurist concept.

When seeking out a partner, try to identify someone who "isn't like you". This doesn't necessarily need to be demographically different per se, but you should look for someone who doesn't view the world in the same way as you. Perhaps they are a bit more of a skeptic, or maybe they're more quantitative than you, or they studied drama when you studied engineering. The point is having differently wired brains interacting together can multiply brain power by limiting some of the overlap and redundancies built in by having similar viewpoints and lower the chances of creating an echo chamber.

The Wisdom of Raj

During my time as a junior staff member at my first consulting firm, I was fortunate to work for several years under a Managing Director[82] named Raj. I believe that in a different life, Raj would have made a wonderful professor or career counselor. Always eager to impart not just work and professional wisdom, but also personal theories on everything from the how to specialize in your career to the merits of arranged marriages[83].

Raj was an incredible person to be working side-by-side with during a formative time in my personal and professional life. More than anyone I've worked with, I remember more

---

[82] Read "big boss man"
[83] His theory was that if you have time on an x-axis and "love" on the y-axis, a relationship tends to follow a predictable bell-curve shape no matter how strong the relationship is. In a western "love" marriage, weddings tend to take place at the peak of love, and then when the relationship starts to go down, people "blame marriage" as the culprit. In an arranged marriage, you get married right at the start so when the relationship plateaus you are less inclined to blame it on the act of marriage and work to find a solution. He would share this theory with anyone that would listen and draw the curve anywhere – whiteboards, notebooks, napkins at restaurants. Agree or not, it's an interesting theory.

kernels of wisdom from Raj. One of those pieces of advice was around building a team. Consulting is notorious for plucking people that are available for projects that may not be the perfect fit and encouraging them to "figure it out" as they go (usually put more professionally than that).

Raj was much more methodical in his approach to developing a team, and during a challenging time finding the right person for a role, he said to me (paraphrased):

> *"I think of the people in my network as a toolbox, and you have to make sure they are the right tool for the job. I don't try to hammer a nail in with a screwdriver; you're not going to get the value out of it and you're going to break the tool. It's your fault if you bring in the wrong person to a job."*

If you are blessed to grow your futurist following and cohort beyond a single partner, make sure to build your team of debaters, ideators, and devil's advocaters. Avoid selecting the people you are closest and most comfortable with. Don't be lazy and ask a non-quantitative person to suddenly build advanced analytics and statistical models. Instead source those that best augment your weaknesses and provide additional tools you do not have at your disposal.

This may require you to "get comfortable with being uncomfortable" around new people that may challenge you and not gel perfectly with your personality, but the benefits will be enormous. I have worked with countless people who may not be invited to my wedding, but damned if I need someone to poke holes in my idea, I'm going to them.

Ideation Requires Variation

Once you find partners, you can facilitate dialogue and discourse in any number of ways, but for the sake of driving creative thought, try and mix things up. I tend to do a ton of whiteboarding when I'm working with an idea[84]. While whiteboarding works for me, it also makes me feel safe, so sometimes I challenge myself to try and communicate a message or discussion differently. Frankly, during COVID-19, it became a bit of requirement as I was unable to convey a message without photographing said whiteboard and texting it to someone (not the most intelligent option out there).

A co-worker introduced me to a website/app called Stickies.io that facilitates structured rounds of, well, sticky

---

[84] I installed a 6-foot, glass whiteboard in my apartment that everyone thought was ridiculous until COVID-19 hit and everyone was working from home – now I'm a genius.

note boards that you populate in a digital atmosphere, then cross-pollinate, and build on each other's ideas in successive rounds. This can be incredibly effective. In one such 20 minutes session, a 30-person team identified and refined about three dozen solid perspectives about what we should do about troublesome product problem.

This is just one of many directions you can take to keep things interesting, but it is important to break routine in both the physical and digital worlds[85]. Routine is efficient, but ideation is not. So, once you find your team, make sure to experiment with the method and approaches.

While there are likely frameworks you can find from any number of authors or blogs, remember that in the practical world, weird scenarios bring about weird ideas, which is what you're going for. Remember, there is someone's job at Lego to sit in an empty, white room and just think of new products[86]. If that's your method, then do that – but if you

---

[85] Other apps that can be used to facilitate digital ideation include: Miro, Ideaflip, Stormboard, POP – the list goes on. These all can translate into live, in-person exercises with sticky notes, string, grids, you name it – they just can get a bit messier:

"20 Best Online Tools for Design Thinking". *SessionLab*. 19 March 2019. https://www.sessionlab.com/blog/design-thinking-online-tools/. (accessed 9 August 2020).

[86] I'm not actually sure this one is true even though I swear I heard it somewhere. I tried Googling endlessly to confirm it but could not. Regardless, I can still imagine it as someone's job.

want to refine the idea, you'll need to bring someone into the white room with you.

CHAPTER 8:

NEVER SAY NEVER

My Origin Story

I have always been a night owl. On most days, my body crashes around 3 or 4 PM – at which point I either need a cup or two of coffee to keep me going or a 20-minute nap. By the time 10 or 11 PM rolls around however (nap or not), I am usually wide awake. This has always been the case for me, and while inconvenient, I believe I would be a better functioning professional if I could ditch the traditional 9 to 5 for something more like an 11 to 7. Or better yet, I could just move to Spain where a mid-day nap may be a bit more socially acceptable.

My impractical sleep schedule was particularly true in my mid-teens. On one such evening when I was sixteen – I really couldn't sleep. This was before streaming video and YouTube and Facebook and iPhones and Instagram – you get the point. Options were limited, so I turned on the TV and started flipping through channels in bed. At 1 AM there wasn't much on beyond infomercials, so it was a tiring slog trying to find something to distract me.

Reluctantly, on that night, I ended up landing on a rerun of *Star Trek: The Next Generation*. I had a preconceived notion about *Star Trek* at the time that was hard to overcome. A show for "nerds" and "losers", I had never really wanted to be a part of it (I was in nerd denial at the time). But as I said, options were limited.

This was when I met Jean-Luc Picard. A man, albeit fictional one, that would have quite a bit of impact on the rest of my life. I do not recall which episode played at the time, but I was enthralled right out of the gate, and it soon became my late-night ritual. I've since watched every episode at least 3 times, and with each new viewing, I garner some lesson that I had previously missed because I was not yet mature enough to "get it".

To Boldly Go

For those less acclimated to the *Star Trek* universe, Jean-Luc Picard is the Captain of a starship called Enterprise in roughly the year 2364. Its mission as outlined during the voiceover of each episode is to *"explore strange new worlds, to seek out new life and new civilizations, to boldly go where no one has gone before..."*. The premise itself is literally the stuff of the future, and its plots have given way to imaginations of the future for all things medical, scientific, engineering, and even philosophical.

Pages upon pages of this book could be dedicated to how the devices featured on the show have inspired generations of technology that we see today in our everyday lives or are being developed. The organization XPRIZE, led by notable futurist Peter Diamandis, even sponsored a contest in 2014 to develop a real life "tricorder" – one of the most prominent medical devices in the *Star Trek* universe. As a result, there was an international competition and the awarding of almost $4 million in funding as well as a nudge in medical technology[87]. But I didn't bring up *Star Trek* to discuss the tech itself, I brought it up to discuss Jean-Luc Picard and his embodiment of futurist ideals.

Portrayed by Patrick Stewart, Captain Picard is a complex man. Noted for his direct orders with phrases such as *"make it so"* and *"engage"* but also for his softer side not limited to respect for human emotions, love of earl grey tea, and a passion for playing an interstellar variation of the flute. Throughout the series he often breaks his own rules, contradicts himself, and strategically bluffs to outmaneuver

---
[87] "Empowering Personal Healthcare." *XPrize*. https://tricorder.xprize.org/prizes/tricorder. (accessed 9 August 2020).

opponents. But perhaps his most notable attribute is his resolve and belief that all things are possible. Exploring the final frontier requires an open mind. When encountering a species that proclaims it can read minds, he sides with it being possible rather than impossible, fighting an instinct us Earth-bound 21st century folks might jump to.

On one occasion, when challenging a crewman (who happens to be an android) to figure out a technical solution to a particularly troubling situation, the crewman proclaims that this may be "impossible". Captain Picard without a moment's hesitation rebuttals *"things are only impossible until they are not!*[88]*"* If *Star Wars* is more your fancy, this statement is close to Han Solo's famous *"Never tell me the odds!"*.

Never is a "No-No" Word

The point here is that when embarking on the futurist voyage, it is easy to throw out phrases that include the words "never" or "impossible". But history has proven time and time again that "never" is a phrase that will come back to haunt you. Pundits and people you will encounter while you

---

[88] "For Captain Picard, THINGS ARE ONLY IMPOSSIBLE UNTIL THEY'RE NOT!" *YouTube.* https://www.youtube.com/watch?v=7-Q9CxKtZUA. (accessed 9 August 2020).

workshop your futurist ideas will often default to a "never" mentality, but you must not do so in return. "Never" (and other absolutist statements about the future) are cheap, dismissive, and will limit your vision. Instead consider more exploratory responses that won't result in embarrassing quotes such as these:

- "There will NEVER be a bigger plane built."
  -- *A Boeing engineer, after the first flight of the 247, a twin-engine plane that holds ten people.*

- "There is NO REASON anyone would want a computer in their home."
  -- *Ken Olson, president, chairman and founder of Digital Equipment Corp., 1977.*

- "To place a man in a multi-stage rocket and project him into the controlling gravitational field of the moon where the passengers can make scientific observations, perhaps land alive, and then return to earth—all that constitutes a wild dream worthy of Jules Verne. I am bold enough to say that such a man-made voyage will NEVER occur regardless of all future advances."
  -- *Lee De Forest, American radio pioneer and inventor of the vacuum tube, 1957*

> **PRINCIPLE #8 – NEVER SAY NEVER**
>
> Futurism requires a person to imagine a world that does not exist and will not for a decade or maybe even century. It is easy to stop yourself, and others, with absolute statements. Achievements that occur today would "never" have been possible 30 years ago. Always maintain an open mind to new ideas and the suggestions your critics may have. Never (irony I know) shut down a discussion.

Beyond Impossible

In 1993, the *Boca Burger* was created. It was not the first "vege-burger" or meatless meat to be produced, but it was the one I was most familiar with from childhood[89]. I wasn't raised vegetarian but had on occasion given it a try. It wasn't very good. Since then I had continued to dabble here and there with an occasional tofu hot dog or vegan chili, but disappointment (an understatement) always followed.

---

[89] "The History of the Veggie Burger". *The Smithsonian Magazine.* 19 March 2014. https://www.smithsonianmag.com/arts-culture/history-veggie-burger-180950163/. (accessed 9 August 2020).

By 2002, *Boca Foods Company* had peaked with about $70 million in sales[90]. While nothing to slouch at, such figures barely put a dent in the $20+ billion in sales *Tyson Foods* alone had around the same period[91]. The challenge it seemed was not a desire to emphatically consume animals, it was the taste. It had seemed that making a vegetable convincingly taste like meat was impossible, and we'd "never" see the day in which people swapped out their meats for tasty substitutes.

Enter *Beyond Meat* seven years later. Fueled by a desire to achieve the impossible (something their rival *Impossible Foods* has inserted directly into their moniker), *Beyond Meat* had a dogged persistence to overcome the history of failures before them. Three years later, they pitched a product to *Whole Foods*. What was to be a major milestone in the company's timeline to market, ended in a failure. But this only doubled *Beyond Meat*'s resolve.

According to an interview with the *Beyond Meat*'s CEO Ethan Brown:

---

[90] I'm nothing if not consistent:
https://en.wikipedia.org/wiki/Boca_Burger
[91] "Tyson Food Revenues 2006 – 2002".
https://www.macrotrends.net/stocks/charts/TSN/tyson-foods/revenue.
(accessed 9 August 2020).

[After getting rejected from Whole Foods] we went back to the lab for four years and worked our asses off, [we] brought in scientists from every angle we could think of--biochemists, protein chemists--to understand meat better than anybody else....we took a model from clean energy, which was get the best scientists, best engineers, fund them well, get them together, give him a clear goal and go for it. And, I knew that was not being done in the food industry." [92]

If you've followed the news or looked on a store shelf lately, you'll see that they have now achieved what was once a "never" on everyone's lips. Their product can be seen not only at *Whole Foods*, but at *Del Taco, Carl's Junior, Dunkin', KFC, A&W, TGIFridays*, and more added every month.

Launching a successful IPO in May 2019, *Beyond Meat* was valued at approximately $8.4 billion as of April 2021. *Beyond Meat* took on a task that had been thought to be

---

[92] Ferenstein, Gregory. "An Interview with the CEO of Beyond Meat". *Forbes*. 26 May 2019.
https://www.forbes.com/sites/gregoryferenstein/2019/05/26/an-interview-with-the-ceo-of-beyond-meat/#1fc789ca7e2a. (accessed 9 August 2020).

impossible and seems to have won. It is now focused on perhaps the "final frontier" for meat lovers. Bacon[93].

Never in the Day to Day

"Never" is among my least favorite words, perhaps barely nudging out the word "luck". The type of "never" imagination limiting mindset is not just reserved for the famous quotes from earlier or *Star Trek* episodes. In my life and work, I have encountered the opposite of the Picard mindset on an almost weekly basis.

On a notable occasion, I was advising a retailer about their interest of entering into a new market. Over the course of several weeks, I did the diligence of talking to their staff, pouring over their data, and reviewing their objectives. There was a path to where they wanted to go, but it was going to cost them. They hadn't invested in the space over the years, and they had ground to make up for.

When I presented my findings, their response was that that level of investment was "never" going to happen. They also thought that their competitors would "never" be willing to

---

[93] "Beyond Meat is working on fake bacon and steak". *CNN.* 24 July 2019. https://www.cnn.com/2019/07/24/business/beyond-meat-bacon-steak/index.html. (accessed 9 August 2020).

outspend them, so they were safe to go about business as usual. Well, guess what, they have yet to (see how I didn't say never) achieve their goals. Also, one of their competitors was willing to do the "impossible", and now they're up against the wall even more than before.

As a forward-thinker or a company with ambition, it is important to be open to other ideas, including critics of your own (do not end up like Dawkins). For budding futurists, please resist your inclination to reject the ideas of others. On the flip side, try to resist some of the never talk in your own minds about what might be possible in the distant future. To quote the 2010 action/sci-fi flick *Inception*, "*You mustn't be afraid to dream a little bigger, darling.*"[94]

---

[94] If you've somehow managed to live under a rock and not see this film yet, you must. I know the visionary mind of Christopher Nolan has some awesome futurist ideas locked up in it.

CHAPTER 9:
PREPARE FOR AND LEARN FROM MISTAKES

Professorial Wisdom

In 2014, after completing the core curriculum during my graduate degree, I was eager to sign up for the elective courses that truly piqued my interest. The core classes were a bit too structured and overly linear for my taste, but the promise of creative, hands-on, and more abstract classes available following the first semester was what gave me the strength to push through topics like Accounting (sorry CPAs).

UCLA has a bidding system for courses, and in winter quarter of that year, I put all my points available down on a course called *"Managing Disruptive Technologies"*. The course was taught by Brian Farrell, the former Chairman and CEO of the gaming company *THQ*. While at *THQ*, Brian successfully grew the company from a $19 million to $1 billion in sales in a little more than a decade[95]. It was an

---

[95] "Brian Farrell". *UCLA Anderson School of Management.* https://www.anderson.ucla.edu/faculty-and-research/marketing/faculty/farrell (accessed 9 August 2020).

exciting opportunity to learn from his experience in a sector I have always been fascinated by and spent hours upon hours in my basement as a child but rarely came across another professional working in the field, let alone an executive.

When I signed up for the course, I had envisioned the class to be very head in the clouds ethereal talk about how rapidly the world is changing. And while there was content which addressed these elements, the focus of the curriculum was on taking a methodical approach to addressing the ever illusive and so often thrown out buzzword of "disruption".

An advocate of some of the disruption frameworks and organizational structure provided by famous Harvard professor Clayton Christensen, our coursework focused on how to be systematic about analyzing leaps in technological and organizational paradigms. Having been the leader of a major gaming institution, however, Professor Farrell brought something many academics do not bring to the table: real-world experience. Being taught Finance or Accounting by a lifetime academic was one thing but being taught by a CEO that led a company that got disrupted *(spoiler alert)* was a whole other experience.

Plan and be Humble

Brian is a very approachable person. During class, I always thought he reminded me of Craig T. Nelson from the 90s television show *Coach* in both aesthetic and tone. In class, when posed with any student's challenging opinion, Professor Farrell would always seek to get the student to realize another way of thinking rather than force feeding answers or shut down dialogue, and he made himself accessible outside of class as well. On one occasion, I asked him to accompany me for a beer after class at one of the local bars, and he obliged me (and even picked up the bill – what a guy).

When he and I spoke for this book, he described his draw into the gaming sector. After graduating from UCLA, Brian made his way into the sector because he had always been interested in the intersection between media and technology, and once there, he was exposed to a constantly changing and highly competitive gaming landscape, which he says was always exciting.

While there were several challenges facing *THQ* in the early '10s, one we discussed in greater detail was *THQ*s involvement in mobile gaming. During the flip phone era,

THQ was the second largest seller of hand-held games (behind *Nintendo*). Brian and *THQ* knew that cell phones were poised to be industry disruptors and as such created an entire wireless gaming division. The rationale was simple – it should be cheaper and easier to build games on flip phones than any console, traditional handheld, or PC. As it turns out, while in some ways it was easier, the financial payoff was simply not there, and they canned the division and swore off the entire mobile market.

Unfortunately, when the iPhone hit several years later, the equation had changed, but *THQ* had already decided that the market was not lucrative and stayed the "no mobile" course. This, Brian will admit, was the wrong choice. They had anchored in on a prior analysis without recognizing new factors and learning from the previously failed endeavor. The world had changed around them, and they hadn't realized that the drivers keeping mobile phone games unprofitable were gone. They had learned the lesson now, but it was admittedly a tough blow to the organization and too little, too late.

Coaching through Disruption

In addition to teaching disruption at UCLA, Professor Farrell helps advise budding entrepreneurs within the MBA program. Some of his key advice for all the teams he helps coach[96] is that while it is important to have vision and use intuition, you cannot ignore facts and need to have the humility to respond in light of information that does not adhere to your hypothesis. Also, while tempting to go "all in" as an entrepreneur, people need to set some funds and resources aside for the next take, so you can apply lessons learned and get it right the next time.

While futurists may not be faced with some of the financial pressures to "get it right", this wisdom is still quite sound. As a visionary, you're going to get some things wrong from time to time, but it is important to learn from them, stay humble, seek outsiders to shake up your world, and save a little energy and credentials to modify your position. You don't want to go "all in" on a stinker of an idea and now no one will listen to your next musing.

---

[96] I swear the fact that he reminds me of Craig T. Nelson from *Coach* is unrelated to the fact that he helps coach students, but I nevertheless recognize the coincidence.

> **PRINCIPLE #9 – PREPARE FOR AND LEARN FROM MISTAKES**
>
> As a futurist, it is expected for you to make informed, confident hypotheses about the world and events around you, but as much research, planning, and hustle you put into it, you're going to be wrong from time to time. While these missteps can be disheartening, you need to try to learn from the errors and incorporate the new knowledge into your next projection. Spreading some of the risk of going "all in" on one big idea is probably a wise idea as well just in case that idea falls apart.

Wii Were Wrong

When the *Nintendo Wii* was released in 2006, I thought it was the idea that would bury the company. With over 100 million units sold, I will confess I was wrong[97]. Similar to what Brian and *THQ* experienced in mobility, I had anchored in a previous history of what had occurred the last time *Nintendo* tried to break the standard console mold with the failed *Virtual Boy* in 1995. But gaming technology had

---

[97] "Nintendo's unit sales of video game consoles 1997 – 2020". *Statista.* 14 July 2020. https://www.statista.com/statistics/227012/lifetime-unit-sales-of-nintendos-home-consoles/. (accessed 9 August 2020).

come a long way since then, and *Nintendo* was poised to launch a whole new wave of immersive gaming that *Microsoft* and *Sony* would later fight desperately to mimic and paved the way for the now seemingly here to stay VR and AR gaming world.

While I was off with the mark here, I still learned valuable lessons about human psychology and entertainment trends that have made me more accurate in my predictions going forward. As a futurist, you do not need to be right 100% of the time – this is impossible[98]. What you do need to do is be open to learn and adjust your perspective based on new information. I think making futurist predictions is a bit like playing a videogame. The first time you "die" in a game you don't hang it up – you've now learned about a roadblock or challenge, and you're better prepared for the next encounter.

I have been wrong in my career on quite a few occasions, but I've always searched for a learning to make me better for the next project. Nobody[99] is perfect, but everyone can learn from mistakes. I'll sometimes look back on some predictions from the past and think "Wow, how dumb were

---

[98] Ugh, I know – I used an absolute term. But, I'm going to make an exception because I'm the author.
[99] There I go with the absolutes again.

they to have thought that balloons would be somehow core to our human existence[100]". But, whoever made this bold claim back in the day, probably learned a thing or two from his or her critics. And I got to give them credit for dreaming shamelessly and putting their thoughts out there!

(Postcard prediction and depiction of life in 2000 from the turn of the century)

---

[100] PHEW! – I made it to 100 footnotes!
"Postcards Show the Year 2000". *Paleofuture.* 24 April 2004. https://paleofuture.com/blog/2007/4/24/postcards-show-the-year-2000-circa-1900.html (accessed 9 August 2020).

CONCLUSION: PULLING IT ALL TOGETHER

The CliffsNotes

As with my promise in the introduction to keep things straight and to the point, I'll conclude quickly (and commit to no more footnotes).

Through these chapters, I have outlined what I believe to be the nine core principles to accepting and embracing the role of a futurist:

1. **Put in the work** – if you don't do your homework and have some basis for your ideas, you're just a guy or gal shouting ideas at people and telling them to trust you.
2. **Courage to persistently share your vision** – if you keep your ideas to yourself you won't inspire anyone – but be prepared to face some hurdles along the way.
3. **Eagerness to rally against the status quo** – if you don't seek things that need to be changed and whip up a following to address resistance, it's going to be hard to come up with and produce more than an incremental difference.

4. **Take action** – if you just sit behind a keyboard, it'll be hard to nudge your idea into the future – try and get some skin in the game!
5. **Have fun with it** – if you're too serious, no one is going to want to listen to you – also, it will be boring and hard to stay motivated.
6. **Foster creativity** – if you're not feeding yourself the right inputs to be creative, it will be a major challenge to come up with something original.
7. **Find a partner** – if you're working alone, it's going to be hard to get the idea abrasion necessary to evolve your thinking and take an idea to the "next level".
8. **Never say never** – if you think a brave new idea (or critique) is impossible take note of all the inventions and cures from the past decade that were once pipedreams.
9. **Prepare for and learn from mistakes** – if you think you're always going to be right, you're wrong – be prepared to make missteps but always look for the hidden lesson.

The Final Word

I hope the theme has come through in these chapters that inspiration can be drawn from all types of sources, not just those classically technological and scientific. Futurism inspiration is all around us from art to social justice and women's clothing trends. Novel ideas do not just come from lifetime academics or tech billionaires, they can come from literally anyone. You must trust yourself and know that you have incredible ideas buried underneath years of being told to stay in your lane.

We have explored each step along the futurism journey from inception through evangelization and activation. While each of these chapters merit their own book by a more academic or structured thinker than myself, I hope this book can stand as a primer to the subject matter and get the gears turning a bit to push folks out of their comfort zones.

The process of transforming a wild idea into reality has existed since the beginning of civilization. Early pioneers of technology and progress are often laughed at, mocked, or sometimes thrown in prison (see Galileo), but what sets them apart is their persistence in the face of adversity (see Galileo again) and willingness to shape an idea over time. While not all futurists are persecuted, and many prove to be wrong, the most effective thinkers challenge conventional beliefs in such a way that inspires others to bring fanciful ideas to life.

So next time you have a fleeting idea that comes to you just before you fall asleep or while you're watching a science fiction movie, write it down, share it with others, and build on it. When in doubt, think like a child. Give yourself permission to build mental sandcastles and find shapes in the clouds like you used to do. Then go tell someone about it. And remember, if they laugh and tell you you're silly, you might be onto something.

Today's innovators weren't born disrupting industries, but they probably started as children with some pretty silly ideas…

Printed in Great Britain
by Amazon